C INSTRUMENTS

THE BERKLEE REAL BOOK

ISBN 978-0-87639-082-5

For more info on the Real Book series, including community forums, please visit **www.officialrealbook.com**.

BERKLEE PRESS

Editor in Chief: Jonathan Feist

Senior Vice President of Pre-College, Online, and Professional Programs/
CEO and Cofounder of Berklee Online: Debbie Cavalier

1140 Boylston Street • MS-855BP
Boston, MA 02215-3693 USA

Visit Berklee Press Online at
www.berkleepress.com

Study music online at
online.berklee.edu

Distributed By

HAL•LEONARD®
—A Muse Group Company—
7777 W. Bluemound Road • P.O. Box 13819
Milwaukee, Wisconsin 53213

Visit Hal Leonard Online
www.halleonard.com

Berklee Press, a publishing activity of Berklee College of Music, is a not-for-profit educational publisher.
Available proceeds from the sales of our products are contributed to the scholarship funds of the college.

HARMONIC ANALYSIS

A

B

C

M

N

O

P

Q

R

S

S (cont.)

T

U

V

W

X

Y

ADAM'S APPLE

(LATIN FUNK)

- WAYNE SHORTER

TYPICAL BEBOP HARMONY, WITH RELATIVELY ACCESSIBLE II V I MOTION.

AFTERNOON IN PARIS

AFTERNOON IN PARIS, FEATURING SACHA DISTEL, KOCH RECORDS, 1956.

\- JOHN LEWIS

Cmaj7 C-7 F7 Bbmaj7

Bb-7 Eb7 Abmaj7 D-7 G7b9

1. Cmaj7 A-7 D-7 G7 2. Cmaj7 A-7

D-7 G7 Cmaj7 A-7

D-7 G7 C#-7 F#7 D-7 G7

Cmaj7 C-7 F7 Bbmaj7 Bb-7 Eb7

Abmaj7 D-7 G7b9 (Cmaj7 A-7 D-7 G7)

FINE

EXAMPLE OF AN ODD NUMBER OF LINES IN VARYING SECTIONS.

CHORUS
Abadd2
Bb
Eb
Dbo7
Ab
Abadd2
F-7
Bb
G-7
Dbo7
F-7
1. G7
2. G7
N.C. (PIANO)
INTERLUDE
F7/C
Eb
Bb
C-
F
Bb
Bb7
CHORUS
Eb
Dbo7
Ab
Abadd2
F-7
Bb
G-7
Dbo7
F-7
TO
Bbsus4
Bb
Eb
G-
G-7
Abmaj7
F-7
Bb
D.S. AL
Bb
G7

(SLOW ROCK-BLUES FEEL)
AIN'T NO SUNSHINE
- BILL WITHERS
VERSE
N.C.
A-7
E-7 G
A-7
E-7 G
A-7
E-7
D-7
A-7
E-7 G
A-7
VERSE
A-7
E-7 G
A-7
E-7 G
A-7
E-7
D-7
A-7
E-7 G
A-7
BRIDGE
N.C.

A-7
E-7
G
VERSE
A-7
A-7
E-7
G
A-7
E-7
G
A-7
E-7
D-7
A-7
E-7
G
A-7
E-7
G
A-9
PLAY 3X

A CHALLENGING UP-TEMPO BEBOP TUNE WITH SOME CHROMATICALLY SHIFTING TONAL CENTERS.

AIREGIN

(BOP)

SONNY ROLLINS, SONNY ROLLINS & CO. 1964, BMG ENTERTAINMENT, 1964.

- SONNY ROLLINS

F-7 C7#9 F-7

F9 Bb-7 F7#9 Bb-7

1. Dbmaj7 D-7 G7 Cmaj7

C#-7 F#7 Bmaj7 C-7 F7 Bbmaj7

Bb-7 Eb7 Abmaj7

G-7b5 C7b9 2. Dbmaj7 D-7 G7 C-7b5

F7 Bb-7 Eb7sus4 Ab (G-7b5 C7b9)

ALL BLUES

(MED. BLUES)

KIND OF BLUE, SONY MUSIC ENTERTAINMENT INC., 1959.

- MILES DAVIS

FIRST EIGHT BARS OF VERSE ARE BUILT ON TWO VARIATIONS OF A SINGLE CHORD (A AND Asus4).

CHORUS
E
G
D
A
E
G
D
A
1.
E
G
D
A
B
2, 3.
E
G
D
A
E
G
D
A
TO
BRIDGE
B
F♯
B
F♯
PLAY 3X
A7
A7sus2
SIM.
A7
A7sus2
D5
A7
A7sus2
Dsus2
A7
A7sus2
D5
B7
B7sus2
Esus2
D.S. AL
B7
B7sus2
Esus2
B7
B7sus2
Esus2
B7
B7sus2
Esus2
OUTRO-GUITAR SOLO
E
G
D
A
E
REPEAT AS DESIRED

GOOD FOR LEARNING TO READ CHANGES.

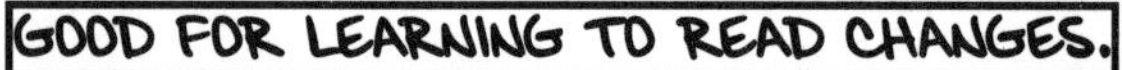

(MED. SWING)

ALL OF ME

LOUIS ARMSTRONG, AMBASSADOR SATCH, SONY MUSIC ENTERTAINMENT INC., 1956.

- SEYMOUR SIMONS/
GERALD MARKS

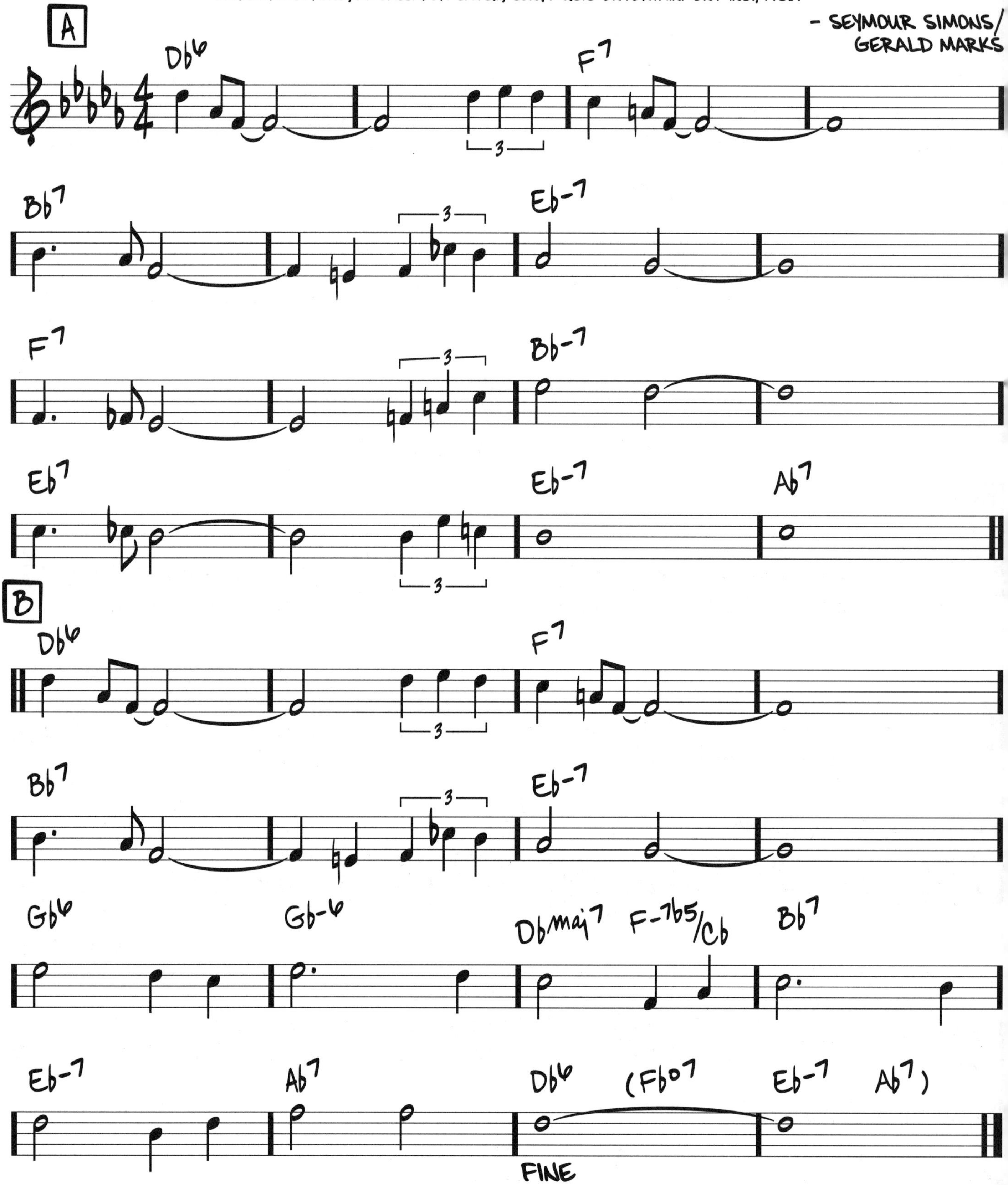
A
Db6
F7
Bb7
Eb-7
F7
Bb-7
Eb7
Eb-7
Ab7
B
Db6
F7
Bb7
Eb-7
Gb6
Gb-6
Dbmaj7
F-7b5/Cb
Bb7
Eb-7
Ab7
Db6
(Fbo7
Eb-7
Ab7)
FINE

BASED ON CHORD PROGRESSIONS FROM THE JAZZ STANDARDS REPERTOIRE.

ALL OF YOU

(MED. SWING)

ELLA FITZGERALD, ELLA FITZGERALD SINGS THE COLE PORTER SONGBOOK, UMG RECORDINGS, 1997.

- COLE PORTER

F-6 CMAJ7 D-7b5 G7b9

F-6 CMAJ7 F-7 Bb7

E-7 Eb°7 D-7 G7

CMAJ7 B7 E-7b5/Bb A7b9 D-7 G7

F-6 CMAJ7 D-7b5 G7b9

F-6 CMAJ7 E-7 A7b9

FMAJ7 F#-7b5 B7b9 E-7 Bb9 A7

D-7 A7 D-7 G7 C6 FINE D-7

AFTER SOLOS, D.S. AL FINE (PLAY PICKUPS)

GOOD EXAMPLE OF A GUIDE-TONE MELODY, MOVING THROUGH MANY HARMONIC AREAS.

ALL THE THINGS YOU ARE

ALONE TOGETHER
(MED. BALLAD)
- HOWARD DIETZ/ARTHUR SCHWARTZ
D-6 E-7b5 A7b9 D-6
E-7b5 A7b9 D-6 A-7b5 D7b9 G-7 D7b9
G-7 B-7 E7 G-7 C7 Fmaj7
E-7b5 A7b9 Dmaj7 1. E-7 A7b9 2.
A-7b5 D7(b13 b9) G-7
G-7b5 C7b9 Fmaj7 E-7b5 A7b9
D-6 E-7b5 A7b9 D-6 E-7b5 A7b9
D-6 B-7b5 Bb7 A7(b13 b9) D-6 (Bb7 A7b9)

ALWAYS BE MY BABY

MARIAH CAREY, DAYDREAM, SONY BMG MUSIC ENTERTAINMENT 1995.

(MED.)

- MARIAH CAREY/JERMAINE DUPRI/MANUEL SEAL

E E/G# Amaj7 A/B C°7

C#-7 E/G# Amaj7 A/B

1. INTERLUDE

E G#-7 Amaj7 A/B E G#-7

2. BRIDGE

Amaj7 A/B C#-7 G#- F# G#

A G#- C#-7 G#- F# G#

A B C

OUTRO-CHORUS

F F/A Bb Bb/C C#°7

D- D-/A Bb Bb/C

F F/A Bb Bb/C C#°7

REPEAT AS DESIRED

D- D-/A Bb Bb/C

ANA MARIA

NATIVE DANCER, SONY MUSIC ENTERTAINMENT, 1975.

- WAYNE SHORTER

C

B-7 | Eb-7

Dmaj7 F7#5 | Bb-7 | Ab-7 | Bb/Ab

G-7 | C7sus4 | Bbmaj7 A-7 | F-7 E-7

G7b9sus4 | Ebmaj9/G | G7b9sus4 | Ebmaj9/G

D SOLOS

G7b9sus4 | Ebmaj9/G | G7b9sus4 | Ebmaj9/G

REPEAT AND FADE

CLEAR CONTRAST BETWEEN SECTIONS AND TITLE EMPHASIS.

ANGEL

(MED. BALLAD)

SARAH MCLACHLAN, SURFACING, BMG, 1997.

- SARAH MCLACHLAN

Gb
Db
Bb-7
Ab7
Ab7sus4
Db
Gb/Db
Db
F-
Gb
Gbsus4
Gb
Db
Bb-7
Ab
1. Db
Gb/Db
Db
Gbadd9/Db
2. Db
Gb
Gbsus4
Gb
Db
OUTRO
Bb-
Ab7
Ab7sus4
Db
Gb/Db
Db
Gb/Db
Db

STANDARD PICKED UP BY MANY JAZZ ARTISTS.
MINOR KEY, AABA FORM.

ANGEL EYES

(SLOW BLUES)

FRANK SINATRA, ONLY THE LONELY, CAPITOL RECORDS, INC., 1958.

– EARL BRENT/MATT DENNIS

GOOD FOR SHOWING II V RELATIONSHIPS, DIATONIC HARMONY, AND MODAL INTERCHANGE.

ANTHROPOLOGY

ART PEPPER +11, MODERN JAZZ CLASSICS, FANTASY, INC. 1959.

AABA FORM.

AS LONG AS I LIVE

LENA HORNE, BLUEBIRD'S BEST: THE YOUNG STAR, BMG, 1972.

(MED.)

- TED KOEHLER/HAROLD ARLEN

(BALLAD)
AUTUMN IN NEW YORK
- VERNON DUKE
G-7 A-7 G-7 C7 Fmaj7 G-7 A-7 D-7b9
G-7 A-7 G-7 C7 A-7b5 D7
G-7 Bb-7 Eb7 Abmaj7 Db7 C-7 G7b9
C-7 Eb7 Abmaj7 G7b9 Cmaj7 A-7 D7b5
G-7 A-7 G-7 C7 Fmaj7 G-7 A-7 D7 Db7
C-7 D-7 Eb-7 F7 Bb-6 Ab-7 Gb7
F-7 C7#5 F-7 E-7 Eb-7 Ab7 Dbmaj7 C7#5 F-7 Ab-7
G-7 A-7 Bb-6 C7b9 F-

GOOD FOR STUDYING MAJOR TO MINOR CHORD PROGRESSIONS, GUIDE TONE MELODIES, MOTIVIC DEVELOPMENT, AND II V I'S.

AUTUMN LEAVES

BILL EVANS, PORTRAIT IN JAZZ (KEEPNEWS COLLECTION), CONCORD MUSIC GROUP INC. 1959.

- JOHNNY MERCER/JACQUES PREVERT/JOSEPH KOSMA

SWING ERA TUNE. AABC FORM, HARMONICALLY SIMPLE, CAN BE PLAYED VERY FAST. TRY IT IN ALL TWELVE KEYS!

AVALON

(MED. UP)

BENNY GOODMAN, LIVE AT CARNEGIE HALL: 1938, SONY MUSIC, 1938.

- AL JOLSON/B.G. DESYLVA/VINCENT ROSE

EXAMPLE OF AN ODD NUMBER OF LINES IN VARYING SECTIONS.

BACK IN THE DAY
(PUFF)

C-9/F
G7#5
Db maj9
C7#9
C-9/F
G7#5
Db maj9
C-9/F
G7#5
Db maj9
C7#9
C-9/F
G7#5
B-/C
D.S. AL ⊕
(TAKE REPEAT)
VERSE
C-9/F
G7#5
Db maj9
C7#9
N.C.
C-9/F
G7#5
Db maj9
C-9/F
G7#5
Db maj9
C7#9
N.C.
C-9/F
G7#5
B-/C
OUTRO
C-9/F
G7#5
Db maj9
C7#9
N.C.
C-9/F
G7#5
Db maj9
C-9/F
REPEAT AND FADE
G7#5
Db maj9
C7#9
N.C.
C-9/F
G7#5
B-/C

BALL AND CHAIN
(SLOW BLUES)
- WILLIE MAE (BIG MAMA) THORNTON
INTRO-SOLO
VERSE
VERSE

Eb7
Bb7
F9
TO
Eb9
Bb7
F7
SOLO
F7
Eb7
Bb7
Eb7
Bb7
F7
D.S. AL
FREELY
Eb9
N.C.
Bb
Bb7/D
Eb
Bb
B9
Bb9

BEAT IT
(MED. FAST ROCK)
MICHAEL JACKSON, THRILLER, EPIC RECORDS, 1982.
- MICHAEL JACKSON
INTRO
N.C. (E-)
(D)
(E-)
1. (D)
2. (D)
(GUITAR)
VERSE
E-
D
(GUITAR SOLO ON D.S.S.)
E-
D
C
D
E-
D
VERSE
E-
D
E-
D
C
D
E-
D
TO ⊕ 2
(GUITAR SOLO ENDS)

CHORUS
E-
D
E-
D
E-
D
E-
TO ⊕ 1
1.
D
E-
D
E-
D
2.
D
D.S. AL ⊕ 1
⊕ 1
D
N.C.
(SYNTH)
(GUITAR)
1.
2.
D.S.S. AL ⊕ 2
⊕ 2
E-
D
E-
D
E-
D
E-
D
REPEAT AND FADE

BASED ON CHORD PROGRESSIONS FROM THE JAZZ STANDARDS REPERTOIRE.

BEAUTIFUL LOVE

SHIRLEY HORN, YOU WON'T FORGET ME, THE VERVE MUSIC GROUP, 1990.

- HAVEN GILLESPIE/VICTOR YOUNG/ WAYNE KING/EGBERT VAN ALSTYNE

BERNIE'S TUNE

GERRY MULLIGAN, PRESENTING THE GERRY MULLIGAN SEXTET, THE VERVE MUSIC GROUP, 1955.

– BERNIE MILLER

CLASSIC BEBOP BLUES HEAD.

BILLIE'S BOUNCE
(BILL'S BOUNCE)

CHARLIE PARKER, MILES DAVIS, BIRDSONG, SAVOY JAZZ RECORDS, 2004.

(FAST BLUES)

- CHARLIE PARKER

F7 Bb7 F7

Bb7 F7

A-7 D7 G-7 C7 TO ⊕ F7 D7

1. G-7 C7 2. G-7 C7 AFTER SOLOS, D.C. AL ⊕ (TAKE REPEAT)

⊕ F7

GOOD EXAMPLE OF A SOPHISTICATED MINOR BLUES TUNE.

BIRK'S WORKS

DIZZY GILLESPIE, THE CHAMP, SAVOY, 1951.

- DIZZY GILLESPIE

BLUESY TUNE WITH INTERESTING BRIDGE AND AABA FORM.

BLACK COFFEE

CHRIS CONNER, CHRIS CONNER AT THE VILLAGE GATE, BLUE NOTE, 2006.

(SLOW BLUES)

- PAUL FRANCIS WEBSTER/SONNY BURKE

HEAVY BASS LINE AND BEAT. JAM SESSION FAVORITE.
(MED. UP JAZZ)
BLACK NILE
NIGHT DREAMER, BLUE NOTE RECORDS, 1964.
- WAYNE SHORTER
INTRO
C-7/F
Gbmaj7
Eb-7
F-7
Bbmaj7
Bb7
Ebmaj7
E-7b5
A7(#9 #5)
HEAD
D-7
Eb7
D-7
C-7
F7#5
Bbmaj7
A7#5
D-7
A7#5
D-7
Eb7
D-7
C-7
F7#5
Bbmaj7
A7#5
D-7
D7(#9 #5)
G-7
C7
F-7
Bb7
Ebmaj7
G-7
C7
F-7
Bb7
Ebmaj7
A7(#9 #5)
D-7
Eb7
D-7
C-7
F7#5
Bbmaj7
A7#5
D-7
(A7#5)
FINE

GOOD EXAMPLE OF MODAL INTERCHANGE, GUIDE-TONE LINES, DIFFERENT MODULATION TYPES.

BLACKBIRD

THE BEATLES, THE BEATLES (WHITE ALBUM), CAPITOL, 1968.

- JOHN LENNON/PAUL McCARTNEY

G/B A7 D7 G F C/E D- C Bb C
F C/E D- C Bb A7 D7
G A7 G/B G
G A-7 G/B C G/B A7 D7sus4
D.C. AL ⊕
⊕ G/B A7 D7sus4 D7 G
C G/B A7 A-7 D7 G

GOOD FOR LEARNING TO READ CHANGES.

CASSANDRA WILSON, LOVERLY, THE BLUE NOTE LABEL GROUP, 2008.

- LUIZ BONFA/ANTONIO CARLOS JOBIM

(MED. BOSSA)

A- | B-7♭5 E7♭9 | A- | B-7♭5 E7♭9

A- | D-7 G7 | Cmaj7 | C#o7

D-7 | G7 | C6 | Fmaj7

B-7♭5 | E7♭9 | A- | B-7♭5 E7♭9

A- | B-7♭5 E7♭9 | A- | B-7♭5 E7♭9 | E-7♭5

A7♭9 | D- | | D-7/C | B-7♭5 E7♭9

AFTER SOLOS,
D.C. AL ⊕

A- A-7/G | Fmaj7 | B-7♭5 | E7♭9 | A- | TO ⊕ B-7♭5 E7♭9

⊕

| D-7 A-7 | D-7 A-7

D-7 E-7 | A- |

GOOD EXAMPLE OF A LINE CLICHÉ IN MAJOR AND MINOR.

GOOD EXAMPLE OF MODULATION AND AMBIGUOUS TONALITY.
AN INTERESTING CHALLENGE TO TRADITIONAL SONG FORM.

NICE DESCENDING BLUES AND TECHNICAL STUDY.

BLUES FOR ALICE

CHARLIE PARKER, BIRD: THE ORIGINAL RECORDINGS OF CHARLIE PARKER, THE VERVE MUSIC GROUP INC. 1988.

- CHARLIE PARKER

MOSTLY DIATONIC HARMONY, I V IV I, MAJOR PENTATONIC SCALE, 2-PART VOCAL, 2-PART GUITAR HARMONY.

BLUE SKY

MED. (MELLOW ROCK)

THE ALLMAN BROTHERS BAND, EAT A PEACH, THE ISLAND DEF JAM MUSIC GROUP, 1972.

- DICKEY BETTS

INTRO

E A 1. A/C♯ D/B add9 A E/G♯ 2. A/C♯ D/B add9 A E/G♯

(GUITAR)

E D A E

VERSE

E B A E B A

E B C♯- A

𝄋 VERSE

E B A E

B A

E (GTRS.) A

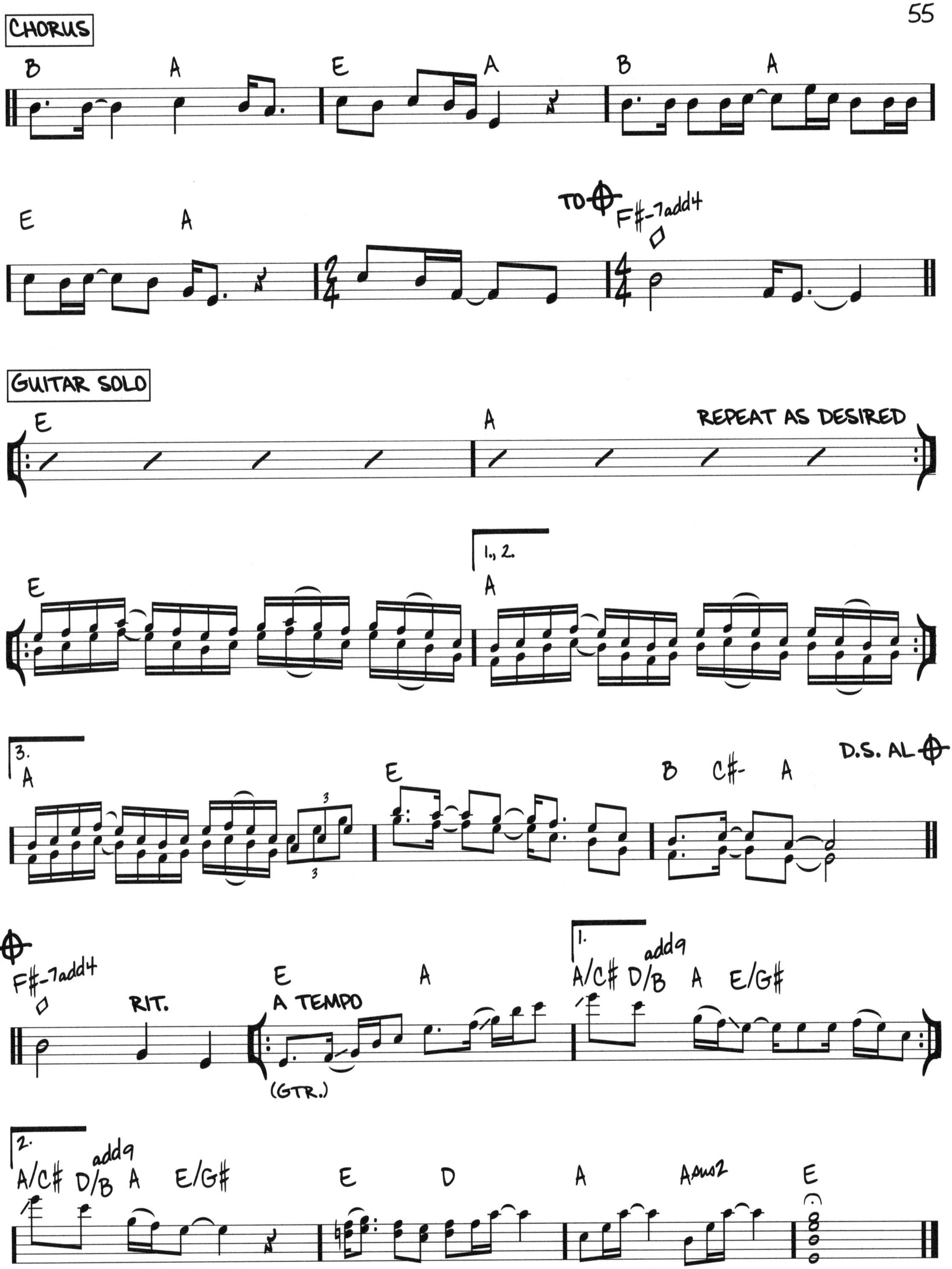

CHORUS

B A E A B A

E A TO 𝄌 F#-7add4

GUITAR SOLO

E A REPEAT AS DESIRED

E 1., 2. A

3. A E B C#- A D.S. AL 𝄌

𝄌 F#-7add4 RIT. E A TEMPO (GTR.) A 1. A/C# D/B add9 A E/G#

2. A/C# D/B add9 A E/G# E D A Asus2 E

(MED.)

BLUES MARCH

- BENNY GOLSON

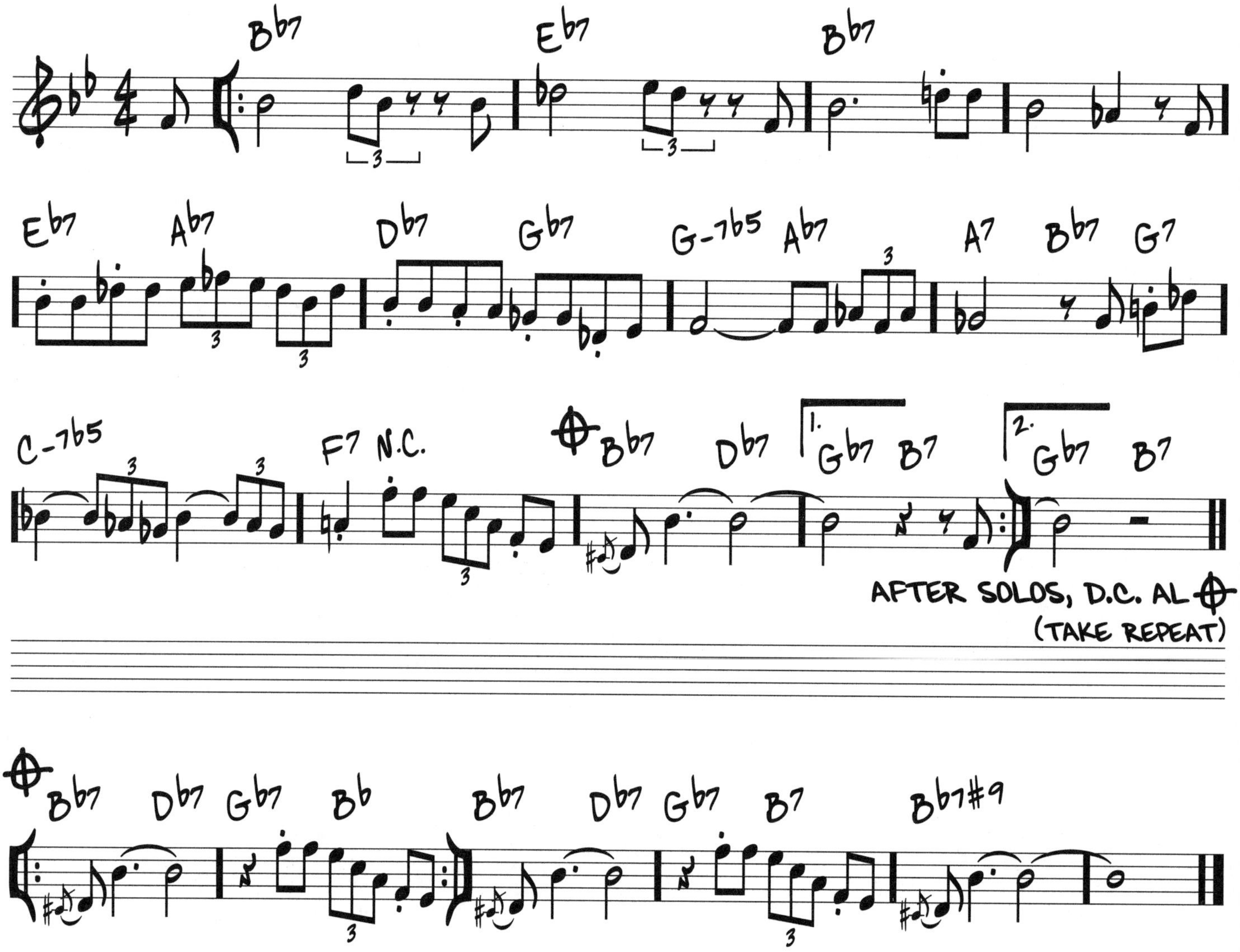

Bb7
Eb7
Bb7
Eb7
Ab7
Db7
Gb7
G-7b5
Ab7
A7
Bb7
G7
C-7b5
F7
N.C.
Bb7
Db7
1.
Gb7
B7
2.
Gb7
B7
AFTER SOLOS, D.C. AL ⊕
(TAKE REPEAT)
⊕
Bb7
Db7
Gb7
Bb
Bb7
Db7
Gb7
B7
Bb7#9

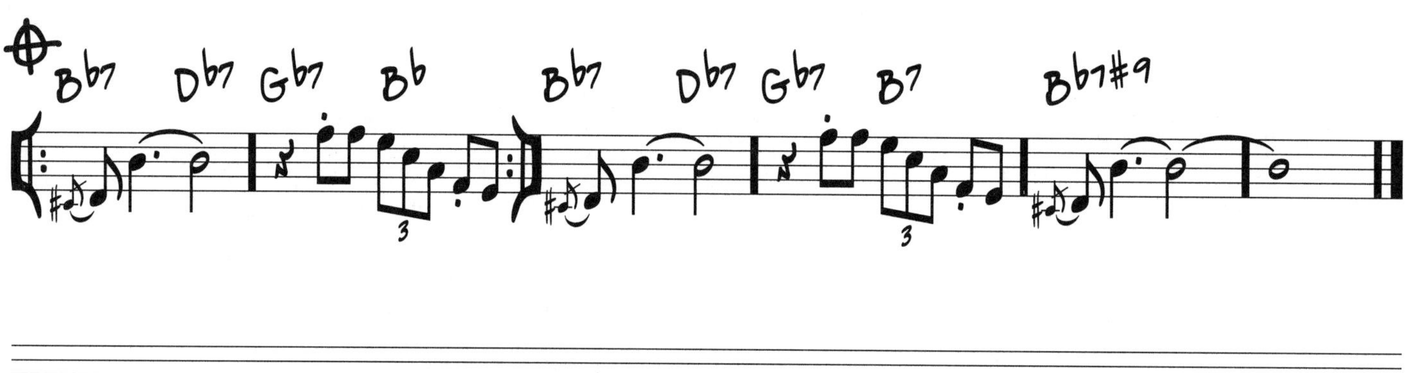

JAZZ WALTZ; EXTENDED BLUES FORM INCLUDING KEY CENTERS THAT ARE CHROMATICALLY DESCENDING.

BLUESETTE

BILL EVANS, PORTRAIT IN JAZZ (KEEPNEWS COLLECTION), CONCORD MUSIC GROUP INC. 1959.

LINE CLICHÉS, HIDDEN REHARMONIZATION.

BODY AND SOUL

COLEMAN HAWKINS, BODY & SOUL, BMG, 1927.

- EDWARD HEYMAN/ROBERT SOUR/ FRANK EYTON/JOHN GREEN

BOLIVIA
(MED.-UP SWING)
- CEDAR WALTON
INTRO
N.C. (G7)
1.,2.,3.
4.
Emaj7
HEAD
Ebmaj7
A13
Dmaj7
Ab7b9
(LATIN)
Gmaj7
F#7#5
B-7
Cmaj7#11
B-7
B-7/A
G#-7b5
(SWING)
G-7
C7
Fmaj7
B7b9
Bbmaj7
A7#9
SOLO ON ENTIRE FORM
(TAKE REPEATS)
ENDING
G7
(VAMP)
ON CUE:
Emaj7
Ebmaj7

EXAMPLE OF VOCAL HARMONIES FROM THE FORTIES.

BOOGIE WOOGIE BUGLE BOY

THE ANDREW SISTERS, APPLE BLOSSOM TIME, ASV LIVING ERA, 2000.

- DON RAYE/HUGHIE PRINCE

VERSE
D *N.C.
*1st X ONLY
(TRUMPET)
G
D
A
G
D
1.
2.
D.S. AL ⊕
(TAKE REPEATS)
D N.C.
(TRUMPET)
G
G#°7
D/A
D

AABA, GREAT BRIDGE, INTERESTING HARMONICALLY, BEBOP-STYLE BALLAD.

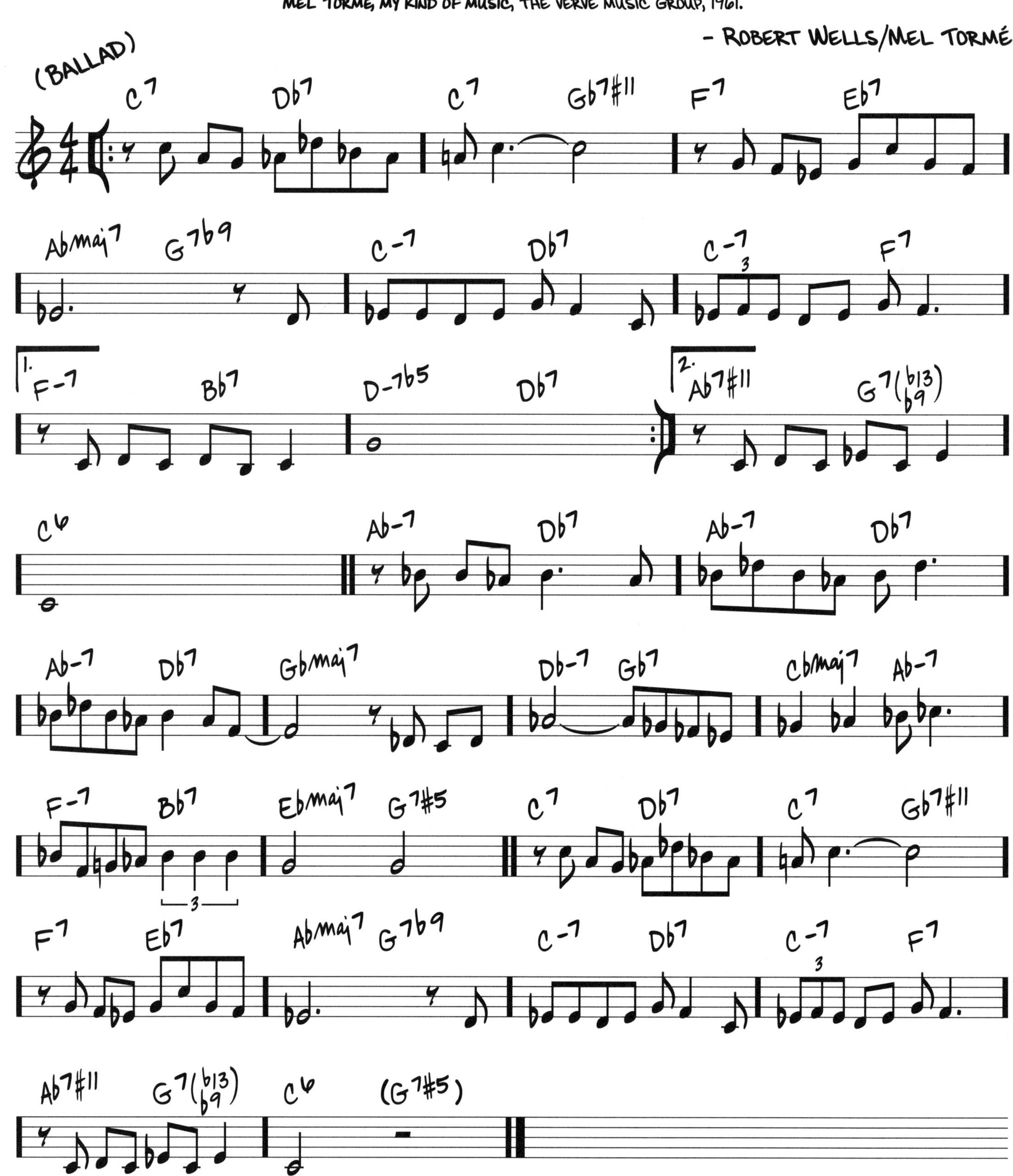

ACCESSIBLE, GOOD FOR LEARNING TO READ CHANGES.

BYE BYE BLACKBIRD

THE COMPLETE COLUMBIA RECORDINGS, MILES DAVIS OR STANDARDS, JIMMY SMITH.

- MORT DIXON/RAY HENDERSON

BREAKIN' AWAY

(MED. SHUFFLE
HALF-TIME FEEL)

- AL JARREAU/JAY GRAYDON/TOM CANNING

Eb7b9
D#-7/G#
G#-7
D#-7
E/F#
F#/E
C
F7sus4
E7sus4
F7sus4
E7sus4
F7sus4
E7sus4
D.S. (TAKE 2nd ENDING)
F7sus4
E7sus4
D
D#-7
G#-7
C#-7
F-7
Bb7b9
Ebmaj7
Eb7b9
D#-7/G#
G#-7
D#-7
E/F#
F#/E
G-7
C-7
C7b9
D#-7/G#
G#-7
D#-7
REPEAT AND FADE

(MED. SLOW)
BREATHE AGAIN
CHORUS
- BABYFACE
C maj7
D-7
E7
F maj7
E-7
A-7
D-7
D-7/G
F
F-6
C
TO
VERSE
F add9
D-9
E-7
A-7
F add9
D-9

E-7
A-7
Fadd9
D-9
E-7
A-7
G-7
C7
Fmaj7
Fadd9
D-9
E-7
A-7
Fadd9
D-9
E-7
A-7
Fadd9
D-9
E-7
A-7
B♭maj7
1. F/G
2. F/G
D.S. AL
F
F-6
C

BREEZIN'

(MED.)

- BOBBY WOMACK

Dmaj9 B-7 E-9 G/A
Dmaj9 B-7 E-9 G/A Dmaj9
B-7 E-9 G/A Dmaj9 B-7
E-9 G/A Dmaj9 B-7
E-9 G/A Dmaj9 B-7
E-9 G/A Dmaj9 B-7
E-9 G/A Dmaj9 B-7 E-9
G/A Dmaj9 B-7 E-9 G/A
Dmaj9 B-7 E-9 G/A
Dmaj9 B-7 E-9 G/A

RIFF BLUES, A GREAT STUDY IN FEELING SYNCOPATION AND SWING.

C-JAM BLUES

DUKE ELLINGTON AND PAUL GONSALVES, DUKE ELLINGTON AND HIS ORCHESTRA FEATURING PAUL GONSALVES, FANTASY, INC., 1962.

- DUKE ELLINGTON

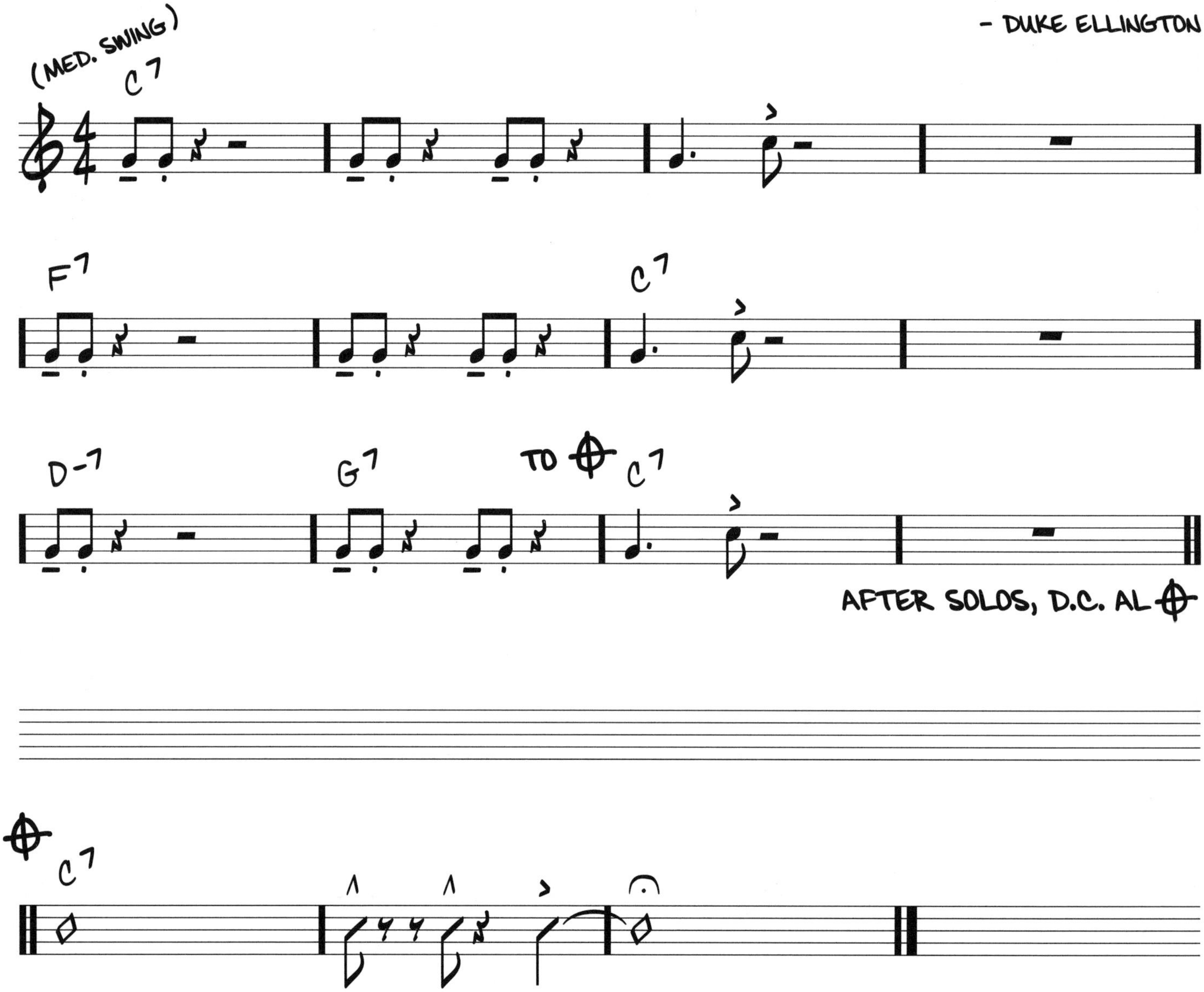

(MED. SWING)

C7

F7 C7

D-7 G7 TO ⊕ C7

AFTER SOLOS, D.C. AL ⊕

MEDIUM JAZZ-FUNK GROOVE THROUGH THREE TONALITIES.

MINOR KEY, WITH GOOD DORIAN SOUND, AABA FORM, RELATIVELY ACCESSIBLE HARMONY AND MELODY.
CARAVAN
DUKE ELLINGTON, MONEY JUNGLE, BLUE NOTE, 1962.
BRIGHT AFRO-LATIN
- DUKE ELLINGTON/IRVING MILLS/ JUAN TIZOL
A (LATIN)
C7
Db7
C7
Db7
C7
Db7
C7
F-6
FINE
B (SWING)
F7
Bb7
Eb7
Ab6
C7
D.C. AL FINE
SOLO A A B A

GOOD EXAMPLE OF HALF STEP/WHOLE STEP SCALE IMPROVISATION OVER MODERN BLUES FORM.

CAREFUL

JIM HALL, *WHERE WOULD I BE?*, FANTASY, INC., 1991.

- JAMES S. HALL

(MEDIUM EVEN 8ths)

A7

D7

A7

F7 E7 A7

1. 2.

A THREE PART SONG: VERSE, TRANSITIONAL BRIDGE, CHORUS, WITH A DIFFERENT MELODY IN EACH SECTION WRITTEN OVER THE SAME CHORD PROGRESSION.

CARELESS WHISPER

WHAM!, MAKE IT BIG, SONY MUSIC ENTERTAINMENT, 1984.

- GEORGE MICHAEL/ANDREW RIDGELEY

CHORUS
D-7
G-7
A-7
Bbmaj7
A-7
D-7
G-7
A-7
Bbmaj7
TO ⊕
1.
A-7
D-7
2.
D.C. AL ⊕
(TAKE REPEAT)
G-7
A-7
Bbmaj7
A-7
A-7
OUTRO
1st X, W/INTRO RIFF
A-7
D-7
AD LIB. TO FADE
G-7
A-7
Bbmaj7
A-7

BOSSA NOVA WITH A CHALLENGING MELODY AND CHORD PROGRESSION.
CEORA
CORNBREAD. 1965.
- LEE MORGAN
(MED. BOSSA)
A
PLAY CUE 2nd TIME ONLY
B
TO
SOLO A B
AFTER SOLOS, D.C. AL
(3X'S)
RIT. (LAST TIME)

R&B CLASSIC WITH GREAT SYNCOPATED BASS LINE. GREAT FOR DEVELOPING SIXTEENTH-NOTE FEEL.
CHAMELEON
(MED. FUNK)
HERBIE HANCOCK, HEADHUNTERS, SONY MUSIC ENTERTAINMENT, 1973.
- HERBIE HANCOCK/PAUL JACKSON/HARVEY MASON/BENNIE MAUPIN
INTRO
N.C.
(BASS)
A
Bb-7
Eb7
BASS CONT. SIM.
B
(PLAY 3X)
N.C.

A NICE LOOK AT THE LYDIAN ♭7 MODE IN ACTION.

CHELSEA BRIDGE

ELLA FITZGERALD, THE COMPLETE ELLA FITZGERALD SONG BOOK, UMG RECORDINGS, 1956.

- BILLY STRAYHORN

A SIMPLE, FRIENDLY MELODY WITHA SIMPLE RHYTHM, GOOD FOR BEGINNING THOSE BURNING TEMPOS. HARDER TO PLAY IN TIME THAN IT LOOKS!

CHEROKEE
(INDIAN LOVE SONG)

CLIFFORD BROWN AND MAX ROACH, STUDY IN BROWN, UMG RECORDINGS, 1955.

- RAY NOBLE

BEBOP BLUES, UNUSUALLY IN THE KEY OF C.

CHERYL

CHARLIE PARKER, BIRD AT THE HIGH-HAT, BLUE NOTE, 1993.

A STRONG MELODIC BALLAD WITH MANY TONAL CENTERS AS WELL AS EXTENDED PEDAL POINT.

CHRISTINA

SOMETHING MORE, IN AND OUT RECORDS, 2005 (1989).

- BUSTER WILLIAMS

STABLE VERSE MOVING TO UNSTABLE CHORUS, SUPPORTING THE IDEA OF THE FREEDOM OF CHILDHOOD.

CHILD AGAIN

BETH NIELSEN CHAPMAN, REPRISE RECORDS, 1990.

- BETH NIELSEN CHAPMAN

INTRO

(SLOW)

B/C♯ E/C♯ B/C♯ | 1. B/C♯ E/C♯ B/C♯ | 2. B/C♯ E/C♯ B/C♯

VERSE

Asus2 Bsus2 | C♯-7

Asus2 Bsus2 | C♯-7

Aadd9 E/G♯ | F♯-7 E/G♯

Aadd9 E/G♯ | F♯-7 A/B

CHORUS

C♯-7 B | Aadd9

C♯-7 B | Aadd9

1. | C♯-7 |

2.
F#-7
Aaddg
F#-7
RIT.
FASTER
Ab
F-
Db
BRIDGE
Eb7sus4
Eb7
Ab
F-
Db
Eb7sus4
Ab
F-
Db
RIT.
A TEMPO
C#-7
B
Aaddg
OUTRO-CHORUS
C#-7
Aaddg
RIT.
C#-7

FUNK STANDARD.

CISSY STRUT

THE METERS, THE METERS, WARNER BROS. RECORDS, 1969.

- ARTHUR NEVILLE/LEO NOCENTELLI/
GEORGE PORTER/JOSEPH MODELISTE, JR.

(MED. ROCK)
COLD DUCK TIME
- EDDIE HARRIS
F7
Bb7
F7
Bb7
F7
Bb7
F7
Bb7
Dbmaj7
Eb(add9)
F7
(FILL)
FINE
1.
2.
AFTER SOLO, D.C. AL FINE
(TAKE REPEAT)

THE CLOSER I GET TO YOU

ROBERTA FLACK, BLUE LIGHTS IN THE BASEMENT, ATLANTIC RECORDS, 1997.

(MED. ROCK BALLAD)

- JAMES MTUME/REGGIE LUCAS

AFTER SOLOS, D.S. AL ⊕
Dmaj7
C♯-7
B-11
E7sus4
⊕ VERSE
Amaj7
Dmaj9
C♯-7
F♯-7
Amaj7
Dmaj9
C♯-7
F♯-7
Amaj7
Dmaj9
C♯-7
F♯-7
Amaj7
Dmaj9
C♯-7
F♯-7
OUTRO
W/VOC. AD LIB.
Amaj7
Dmaj9
C♯-7
F♯-7
Amaj7
Dmaj9
C♯-7
F♯-7

GREAT FOR DEVELOPING TIGHT RHYTHM SECTION SKILL, EMPHASIZING SYNCOPATION (DISPLACED BACKBEAT).

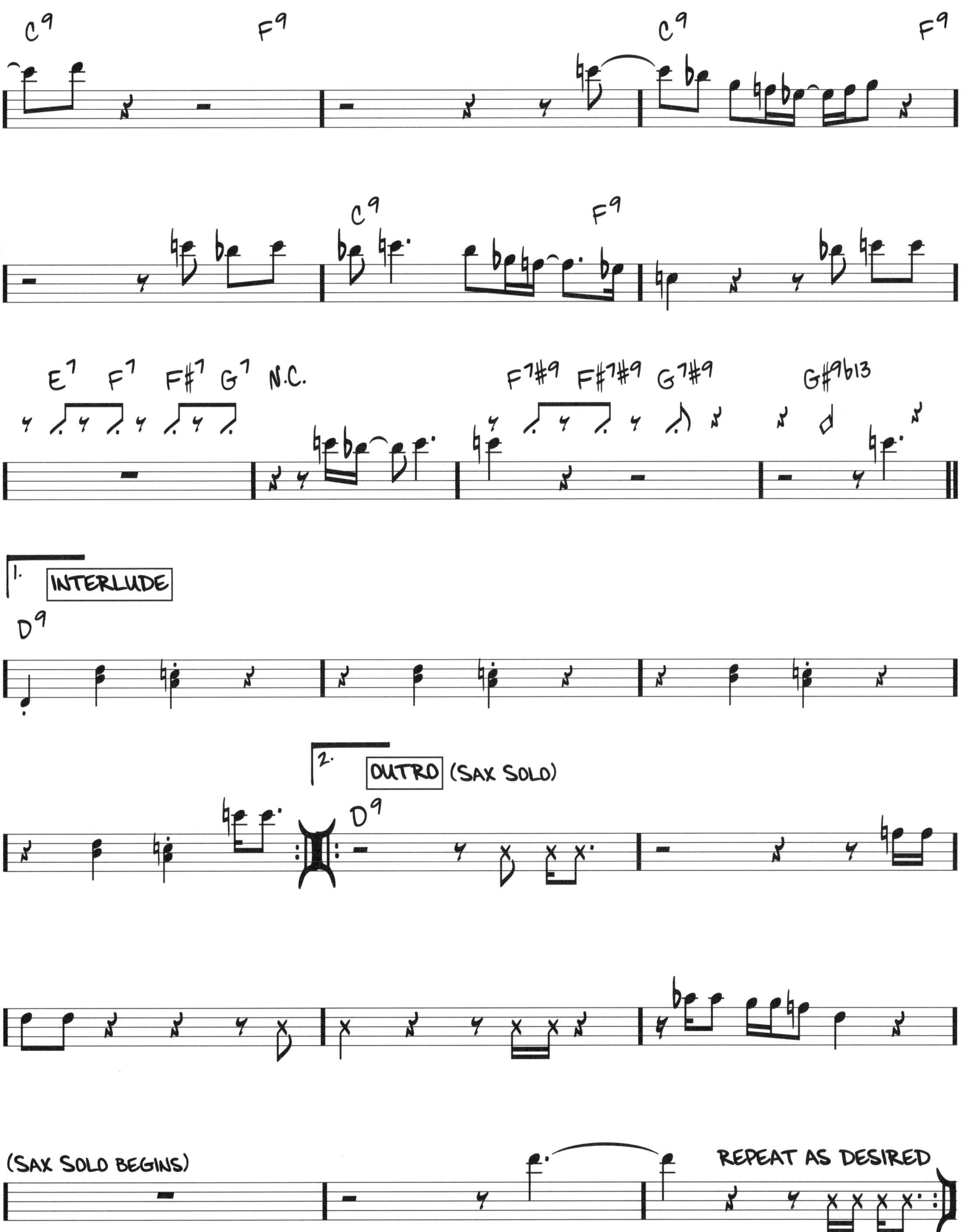

C9
F9
C9
F9
C9
F9
E7 F7 F#7 G7 N.C.
F7#9 F#7#9 G7#9
G#9b13
1.
INTERLUDE
D9
2.
OUTRO (SAX SOLO)
D9
(SAX SOLO BEGINS)
REPEAT AS DESIRED

COME ON IN MY KITCHEN

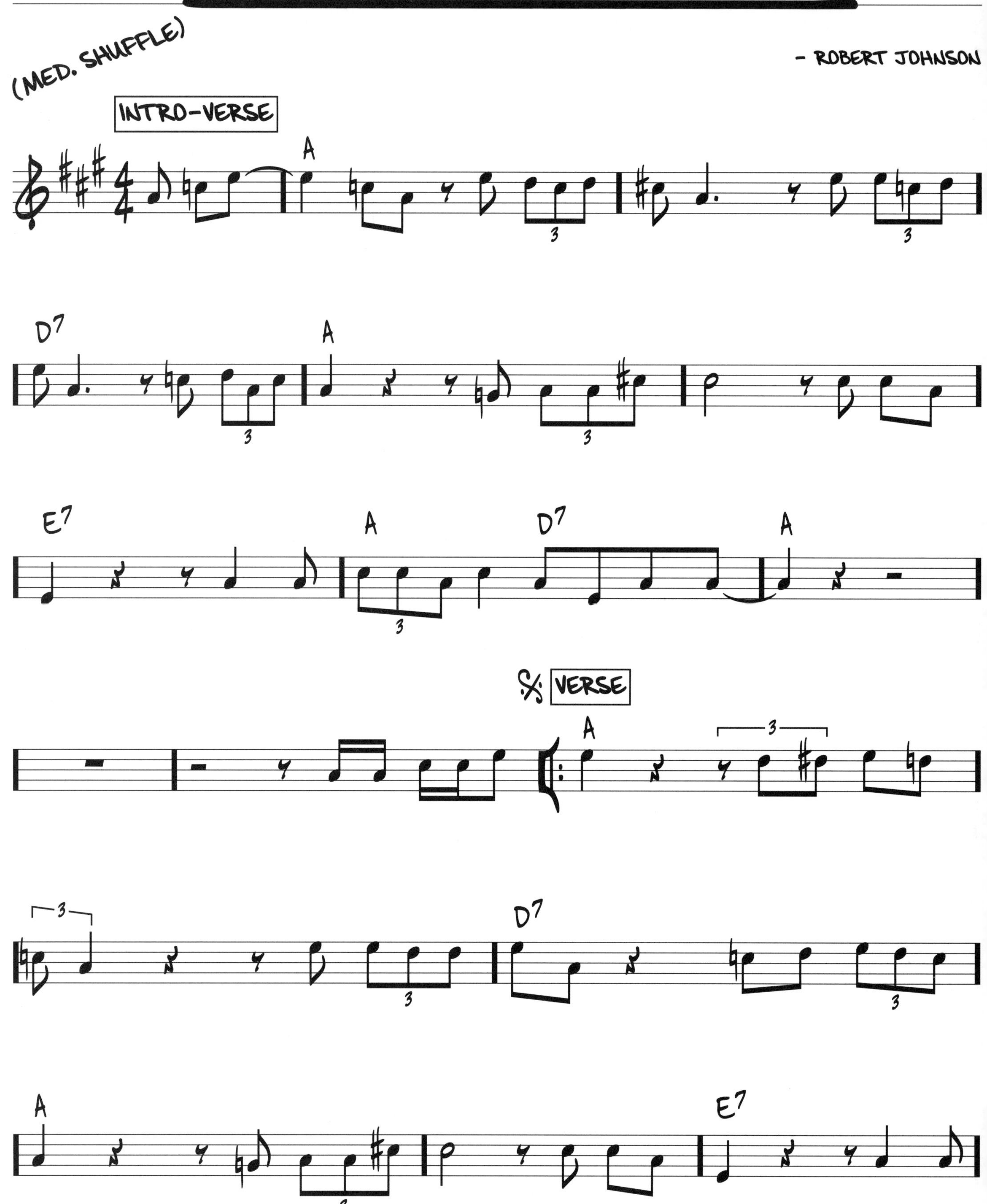

A
D7
TO ⊕
1., 3.
A
3
2.
A
SOLO
A
D7
A
3
E7
A
D7
3
A
D.S. AL ⊕
(TAKE REPEAT)
⊕
A

A BEAUTIFUL, SIMPLE MELODY THAT USES SUSTAINED TENSION DEGREE COLORS ON DOMINANT 7 CHORDS (#11 AND 9, ESSENTIALLY).

COME SUNDAY

FROM BLACK, BROWN & BEIGE

DUKE ELLINGTON, BLACK, BROWN, & BEIGE FEATURING MAHALIA JACKSON, 1958.

- DUKE ELLINGTON

MINOR BLUES WITH A GREAT HARMONIC DEVICE AT THE END (CHROMATIC DESCENDING PATTERN).

COMIN' HOME BABY

HERBIE MANN, WATERBED, ATLANTIC, 1975.

- ROBERT DOROUGH/
BENJAMIN TUCKER

(SOUL JAZZ)

G-7

Eb7

G-7

Bb7

A7

Ab7

G-7

1.

2.

BEAUTIFUL MELODIC USE OF A REPEATED NOTE, ACCOMPANIED NICELY WITH DESCENDING STEPWISE BASS LINE. NICE STUDY FOR CHANGING GROOVES.

CON ALMA

(LATIN)

JAZZ JOURNEYS PRESENTS THE BIRTH OF BEBOP, VOL. 2 (100 ESSENTIAL TRACKS), 2013.

- JOHN "DIZZY" GILLESPIE

INTRO

Db9 C9 Db9 C9

A

Emaj7 G#7/D# C#-7 B7 Bb7 Eb7b5 Ebmaj7 Eb-7 Ab7

Dbmaj7 F7/C Bb-7 Ab7 G7 Db7b5 1. Cmaj7 2. Cmaj7

B

C-7b5 F7b9 F#-7b5 B7b9

Emaj7 F-7 Bb7 B7

3

A

Emaj7 G#7/D# C#-7 B7 Bb7 E7b5 Ebmaj7 Eb-7 Ab7

Dbmaj7 F7/C Bb-7 Ab7 G7 Db7b5 Cmaj7

C
C7b9
Gb
TO ⊕
F-(maj7)
C7
N.C.
SOLO A A B A
PLAY C IN/OUT
AFTER SOLOS, D.S. AL ⊕
F-(maj7)

FUNKY SOUL CLASSIC, WITH STRONG PROTEST LYRIC.

COMPARED TO WHAT

EDDIE HARRIS AND LES McCANN, SWISS MOVEMENT, ATLANTIC RECORDING CORPORATION, 1969.

- EUGENE McDANIELS

REPEAT FOR ADDITIONAL VERSES

THE EPITOME OF BEBOP.

CONCEPTION

THAT SHEARING SOUND, TELARC, 1994.

- GEORGE SHEARING

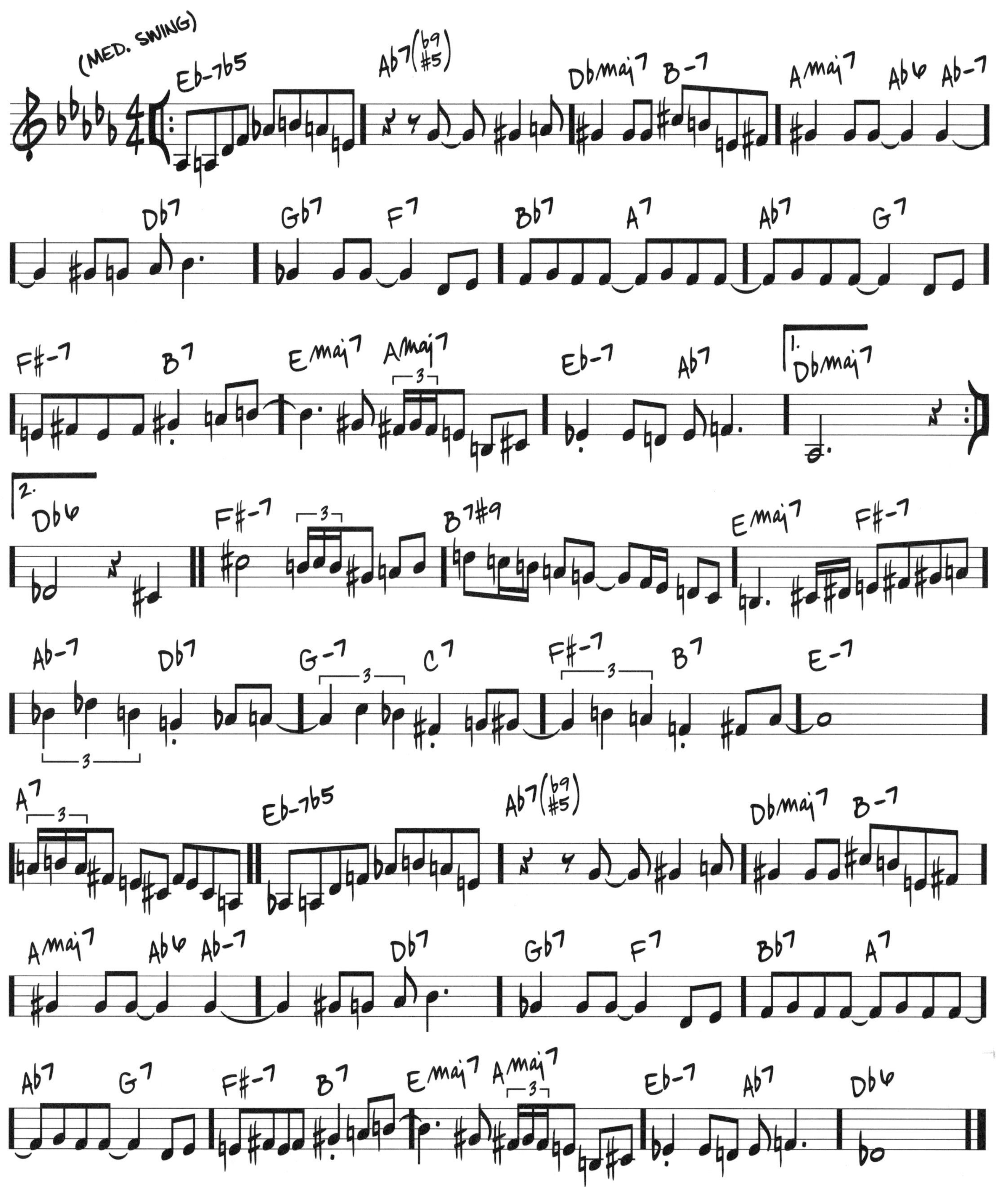

GREAT TECHNICAL STUDY MELODICALLY AND
A GOOD LOOK AT DESCENDING II V'S IN STEPWISE MOTION.
CONFIRMATION
(BOP)
CHARLIE PARKER AND DIZZY GILLESPIE, DIZ 'N' BIRD AT CARNEGIE HALL, 1947.
- CHARLIE PARKER

EXAMPLE OF MODAL INTERCHANGE.

CRYSTAL SILENCE

CHICK COREA AND GARY BURTON, CRYSTAL SILENCE, EMC RECORDS GIMBH, 1972.

- CHICK COREA

CUBAN BALLAD.

CONTIGO EN LA DISTANCIA

G7sus4 G7 C-7 Eb-9
Bbmaj7 Ab7 G7sus4 G7 C-7
F7sus4 F7 Bbmaj7 A-7b5 D7
C
G- G-/F E-7b5 A7 D-7
D-7b5 G7 C-7 F7sus4 F7
D-7b5 G7 C-7 C#-7 D-7
Eb-7 Ab7 Bbmaj7 G-7
C-7 F7 F/Eb D-7b5
G7 C-7 F7
E-7b5 Eb-7 D-7 G7 C-7 F7 Bbmaj7
RIT.

FREE BLUES FORM, WITH IRREGULAR HARMONIC RHYTHM AND LINE CLICHÉ IN THE BASS.

CROSS ROAD BLUES
(CROSSROADS)

KING OF THE DELTA BLUES SINGERS, 1998. COLUMBIA/LEGACY [VIA ALLMUSIC]

- ROBERT JOHNSON

D7
A7
TO
E7
A7
SOLO 12-BAR BLUES
AFTER SOLOS, D.S. AL
(PLAY PICKUP)
E7
A
A/G
A/F#
A/F
A/E
A

DANCE OF THE INFIDELS

(BOP)

- EARL "BUD" POWELL

DAT DERE

(MED. SWING)

- BOBBY TIMMONS

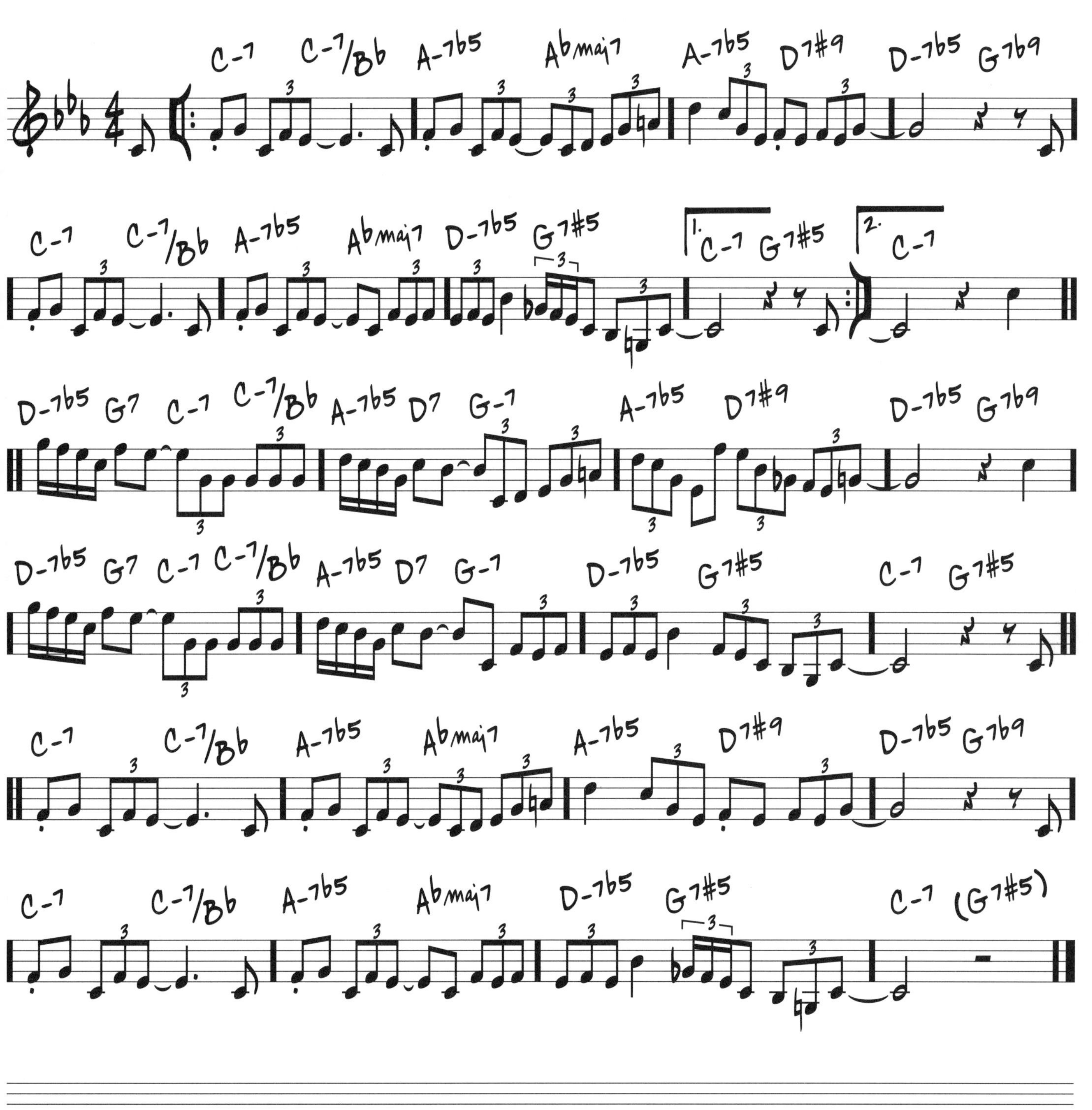

DECEPTIVE RESOLUTIONS OF SECONDARY DOMINANTS TO UNEXPECTED TARGET QUALITIES.

FAST "RHYTHM" CHANGES.

DEXTERITY

CHARLIE PARKER ON DIAL: THE COMPLETE SESSIONS, SPOTLITE RECORDS, 1993.

- CHARLIE PARKER

STRAIGHT AHEAD CHANGES, USED FOR BASIC IMPROVISATION.

DO NOTHIN' TILL YOU HEAR FROM ME

DUKE ELLINGTON AND RAY BROWN, THIS ONE'S FOR BLANTON, PABLO RECORDS, 1972.

- DUKE ELLINGTON/
BOB RUSSELL

SOPHISTICATED HARMONY, THROUGH COMPOSED FORM.
DOLPHIN DANCE
MAIDEN VOYAGE, BLUE NOTE RECORDS, 1999.
- HERBIE HANCOCK
(MED. JAZZ)
Ebmaj7 Dbmaj7/Eb Ebmaj7 D-7b5 G7b9
C-7 Ab7#11 C-7 A-7 D7
Gmaj7 Ab-7 Db7 F-7 Bb7
C-7 C-7/Bb A-7 D7
Gmaj7 D-7/G A/G G7sus4
F7sus4 F7b9 F7sus4 E-7 A7
Eb7 A-7 D7 B-7 E7 D-7
3
3
C#-7 F#7 Dmaj7/E Cmaj7/E Dmaj7/E Cmaj7/E
Dbmaj7/Eb Bb7b9/Eb C7#9/Eb D-7b5 G7b9

I VI II V TUNE WITH REGULAR BRIDGE, WITH RHYTHM-TYPE CHANGES.

DON'T BE THAT WAY

BENNY GOODMAN, DON'T BE THAT WAY, DIGITALPRESSURE/KEM ENTERPRISES INC., 1993.

AABA, 32-BAR FORM, HARMONICALLY STRAIGHT AHEAD, DIATONIC AND SECONDARY DOMINANT CHORDS.

DON'T BLAME ME

CHARLIE PARKER, THE COMPLETE SAVOY & DIAL MASTER TAKES, SAVOY JAZZ, 2002 (1944-1948).

- DOROTHY FIELDS/JIMMY McHUGH

GOOD ILLUSTRATION OF MELODIC SEQUENCE, HYBRID REHARMONIZATIONS, MODAL INTERCHANGE.

(MED. ROCK)

DON'T TAKE ME ALIVE

STEELY DAN, THE ROYAL SCAM, UMG RECORDINGS, 1976.

- WALTER BECKER/DONALD FAGEN

Bb/Eb
C/F
D/G
Eb/Ab
F/G
C-7
CHORUS
(C-7)
F/G
C-7
F/G
G
F
G
F-(add9)
G-(add9)
Ab add9
Bb add9
C 7sus4
Eb/Ab
F/G
C-7
F/G
C-7
F/G
G
F
G
F-(add9)
TO
G-(add9)
Ab add9
Bb add9
C 7sus4
INTERLUDE
G7
C-7
1.
2.
C 7sus4
G/A
F/G
C 7sus4
G/A
F/G
GUITAR SOLO
D.S. AL
C/F
D/G
Eb/Ab
F/G
C-7
Bb add9
F-(add9)
G-(add9)
Ab add9
Bb add9
F-(add9)
G-(add9)
Ab add9
RIT.
Bb add9
C-7
(AD LIB. GUITAR CADENZA)

EPITOME OF FAST BOP.

DONNA LEE

DIZZY GILLESPIE, CHARLIE PARKER: 10TH MEMORIAL CONCERT 3/27/65, VERVE, 1965.

- CHARLIE PARKER

(MED.)
DOXY
- SONNY ROLLINS
Bb7
Ab7
G7
C7
F7
Bb
F7#5
Bb7
Ab7
G7
C7
F7
Bb7
Eb7
E°7
Bb7
Ab7
G7
C7
F7
1. Bb7
F7#5
2. Bb

TRANSITIONAL BRIDGE PROVIDES UNUSUAL HARMONIC INTEREST.

DRIVE

MAKE YOURSELF, SONY MUSIC ENTERTAINMENT INC., 1999.

- BRANDON BOYD/MICHAEL EINZIGER/
ALEX KATUNICH/JOSE PASILLAS II/
CHRIS KILMORE

𝄋 CHORUS

E- E-9 | Cmaj7 A7sus4 | E- E-9

Cmaj7 A7sus2 | E- E-9 | Cmaj7 A7sus4

E- E-9 | 1. Cmaj7 A7sus2 TO 𝄌 | 2. Cmaj7 * A7sus2

* SLIDE GTR.

INTERLUDE

E- E-9 | Cmaj7 A7sus4 | E- E-9 | Cmaj7 A7sus2

E- E-9 | Cmaj7 A7sus4 | E- E-9 | Cmaj7 A7sus2

Cmaj7 A7 | Cmaj7 A7

N.C.

D.S. AL 𝄌
(TAKE 1st ENDING)

𝄌 OUTRO

E- E-9 | Cmaj7 A7sus4 | E- E-9

Cmaj7 A7sus2 | E- E-9 | Cmaj7 A7sus4

E- E-9 | Cmaj7 A7sus2 | Cmaj7 A7

GOOD EXAMPLE OF INTERPOLATED II7, LITERAL MELODIC SEQUENCE, DECEPTIVE RESOLUTION.

EAST OF THE SUN (AND WEST OF THE MOON)

DIANA KRALL, WHEN I LOOK IN YOUR EYES, THE VERVE MUSIC GROUP, 1998.

- BROOKS BOWMAN

SIMPLE RIFF ON A I VI II V PROGRESSION, GOING TO IV ON THE BRIDGE. UNUSUAL ABA FORM.

EASY DOES IT

SONNY STITT & THE OSCAR PETERSON TRIO, SONNY STITT SITS IN WITH THE OSCAR PETERSON TRIO, THE VERVE MUSIC GROUP, 1957.

(MED.)
EASY LOVER
- PHIL COLLINS/PHILIP BAILEY/NATHAN EAST
INTRO
Gbmaj13#11 F-11 Gbmaj13#11 F-11
(KEYS)
Db Eb F-7 Bb-7 C-7 F-7 Db Eb F-7
(GUITAR)
Db Eb F-7
CHORUS
Bb-7 C-7 F-7 Db
(GTR. CONT. SIM.)
Eb F-7 Bb-7 C-7 F-7 Db
Eb F-7 Bb-7 C-7 F-7 Db
3rd X, TO 1
4th X, TO 2
Eb F-7 Bb-7 C-7 F-7
VERSE
Db C- Db C- Db C- Db
Eb F-7 Eb F-7 Eb F-7

C- Db C- Db C- Db C- Db

Eb F-7 Eb F-7 C- F-7

Bb-7 𝄋 BRIDGE C-7 F-7 Bb-7

C-7 F-7 Bb-7

C-7 F-7 Gbmaj13#11 1. Db

(2nd X, KEYS W/ INTRO RIFF SIM.)

Eb F-7 2. F-11

Gbmaj13#11 F-11 Db Eb F-7

GUITAR SOLO

D.S. AL ⊕1 (TAKE REPEAT)

Bb-7 C-7 F-7 Db 1.-3. Eb F-7 4. Eb Bb-7

⊕1 D.S.S. AL ⊕2 ⊕2

Db Eb F-7 Db Eb F-7 N.C.

EXAMPLE OF SUBSTITUTE DOMINANT AND PASSING DIMINISHED CHORDS, AND USING A VARIETY OF VOICING TECHNIQUES.

EASY TO LOVE
(YOU'D BE SO EASY TO LOVE)

ELLA FITZGERALD, ELLA FITZGERALD SINGS THE COLE PORTER SONGBOOK, THE VERVE MUSIC GROUP, 1940.

- COLE PORTER

EMBRACEABLE YOU

DUKE ELLINGTON, FAR EAST SUITE, BMG MUSIC, 1967

- GEORGE GERSHWIN/IRA GERSHWIN

CATCHY HOOK, POWERFUL GROOVE, GREAT FOR GROOVE PRACTICE.

EMOTIONS

A-7 C/G D-7 E7 F/G N.C.
CHORUS
FMaj7 E-7 A-7 FMaj7 E-7 A-7
FMaj7 E-7 A-7 G-7 C7 FMaj7 E-7 A-7
Bb/C F/C C
Bb F Esus4
E FMaj7 E-7 A-7
FMaj7 E-7 A-7 E7/G# D-7 E-7 F/G N.C.
(GUITAR-SIM. ON REPEATS)
OUTRO/CHORUS
FMaj7 E-7 A-7 FMaj7 E-7 A-7
FMaj7 E-7 A-7 G-7 C7 1., 2. FMaj7 E-7 A-7
3. FMaj7 E-7 A-7 N.C.

(BOP)

EPISTROPHY

- THELONIOUS MONK/KENNY CLARKE

MINOR BLUES WITH A REPEATED BASS RIFF/OSTINATO.

EQUINOX

(MED.)

COLTRANE'S SOUND, ATLANTIC WEA, OCTOBER 24, 1960.

- JOHN COLTRANE

E.S.P.
(FAST SWING)
- WAYNE SHORTER
E7(#9 #5)
Fmaj7
Ebmaj7#11
D7#9
E7#9
Ebmaj7
D-7
G7
G-7
Gbmaj7#11
Db7#11
Db-7
Gb7
3
1.
2.
AFTER SOLOS, D.C. AL

TYPICAL AABA FORM, INTERESTING MELODIC TWISTS AND TURNS WHERE THE MELODY ANTICIPATES WHAT HARMONIES ARE COMING UP (HARMONIC ANTICIPATION).

EVERYTHING HAPPENS TO ME

CHET BAKER, JAZZ 'ROUND MIDNIGHT: CHET BAKER, UMG RECORDINGS, INC., 1955.

- MATT DENNIS/TOM ADAIR

MODAL INTERCHANGE, OSTINATO, SOPRANO TONIC PEDAL.

EVERY LITTLE THING SHE DOES IS MAGIC

THE POLICE, EVERY BREATH YOU TAKE: THE CLASSICS, UMG RECORDINGS INC, 1995.

- STING

G6sus2/B G6sus2/C# 2. Bb C/F

BRIDGE

Bb6/9 F6sus2/A G7sus4 F6sus2/A

G7sus4 F6sus2/A Bb6/9 F6sus2/A

Bb6 Csus2 Bb6 Csus2

Bb6 Csus2 Bb6 Csus2 D G A D F#-7

CHORUS

A D A D

A D 1. A D

OUTRO

2. A Bb C/F G-7 A-7 Bb

C/F D

REPEAT AND FADE

(MED.)
EVERYDAY PEOPLE
INTRO
- SYLVESTER STEWART
G
C/G
G
(PIANO)
(BASS)
VERSE
G
C/G
G
C/G
G
C/G
G
C/G
G
CHORUS
C/G
G
C/G
G
3

VERSE
G
C/G
G
C/G
G
C/G
G
C/G
G
C/G
G
3rd X, TO ⊕
C/G
G
2nd X, D.S. AL ⊕
CHORUS
C/G
G
3
N.C.

FALLIN'

(SLOW)

INTRO

- ALICIA J. AUGELLO-COOK

FREELY
N.C.

VERSE
A TEMPO
E- B-7 E- B-7

E- B-7 E- B-7

E- B-7 E- B-7

E- B-7 E- B-7

CHORUS
E- B-7 E- B-7

E- B-7 E- B-7 N.C. TO

VERSE
E-
B-7
E-
B-7
E-
B-7
E-
B-7
E-
B-7
E-
B-7
E-
B-7
E-
B-7
D.S. AL
BRIDGE
E-
B-7
E-
B-7
E-
B-7
PLAY 3X
E-
B-7
CHORUS
E-
B-7
E-
B-7
E-
B-7
1., 2.
E-
B-7
3.
E-
B-7
N.C.
OUTRO
(W/INSTRUMENTAL AD LIB.)
E-
B-7
PLAY 8X
E-

SOPHISTICATED HARMONICALLY.

FEE-FI-FO-FUM

WAYNE SHORTER, SPEAK NO EVIL, BLUE NOTE RECORDS, 1999.

(SWING)

- WAYNE SHORTER

Eb7 D7#9 G-7 Abmaj7 Bmaj7 D7 D-7 G7 3

Eb7 D7#9 G-7 Abmaj7 C7b9 F7 Bb7

Eb7 Bb7

Eb7 Bb-7 Eb7 A-7 D7 3

Eb7 D7#9 G-7 Abmaj7 Bmaj7 D7 D-7 G7 3

Eb7 D7#9 Dbmaj7 C7b9 Bmaj7

FINE

EXCELLENT EXAMPLE OF LATIN.

REPRESENTATIVE OF JOBIM'S STYLE.
A FELICIDADE
(FAST LATIN)
JOE HENDERSON, DOUBLE RAINBOW, POLYGRAM RECORDS, 1995.
- VINICIUS DE MORAES/ANTONIO CARLOS JOBIM
A-7
E-7 B7b9 E-7 A7 D-7 G7
Cmaj7 B-7b5 E7b9
A-7 Ab7 G-7 C9
Fmaj7 Bb9#11 A-7 D7
A-7 B-7 E7(b9 #5) A-7 G7sus4 G7

C maj7
F7
3
3
C maj7
G-7
C7
F maj7
D-7
G7
C6
F#-7b5
3
B7b9
E-7
A7
D-7
G7b9
A-7
A-7/G
D7/F#
D-7/F
A-7
B-7b5
E7(b9 #5)
A-7
1.
2.
A-7

GREAT EXAMPLE OF ACCELERATION USING LINE LENGTH AND INTERNAL RHYME.

FIFTY WAYS TO LEAVE YOUR LOVER

STILL CRAZY AFTER ALL THESE YEARS, WARNER BROS., 1975.

- PAUL SIMON

B7(no3rd)/F#
B+
E-
D6
Cmaj7
B7b9
E-
A-7
E-
A-7
E-
CHORUS
(♩=𝅗𝅥)
G
Bb
C
G
Bb
C
4th X, TO
1.G
2.G
D.S. AL
(TAKE REPEATS)
(DRUMS)
G
N.C.
(DRUMS)

GOOD JAM-BAND TUNE, EXAMPLE OF NEW ORLEANS FUNK.

FIRE ON THE BAYOU

THE METERS, FIRE ON THE BAYOU, ATLANTIC RECORDING CORP., 2005.

- LEO NOCENTELLI/ARTHUR NEVILLE/ GEORGE PORTER/JOSEPH MODELISTE/ CYRIL NEVILLE

CHORUS
D-7
TO ⊕
GUITAR SOLO
D-7
BS. TACET
N.C.
(ORGAN AND BASS)
PLAY 5X
GTR. TACET
D.S. AL ⊕
(NO REPEAT)
⊕ OUTRO-GUITAR SOLO
D-7
BS. TACET
N.C.
REPEAT AND FADE

A NICE IMPROVISING VEHICLE FOR ALL LEVELS THAT CAN BE ARRANGED MANY WAYS FOR RHYTHM SECTION.
FOOTPRINTS
WAYNE SHORTER, ADAM'S APPLE, BLUE NOTE RECORDS, 1966.
- WAYNE SHORTER
(JAZZ WALTZ)
INTRO
C-7
(BASS)
HEAD
C-7
BASS CONT. SIM.
F-7
C-7
F#-7b5
F7#11
E7(b9 #5)
A7(b9 #5)
C-7

AN ASYMMETRIC FORM WITHIN THE CONTEXT OF A STRAIGHT-EIGHTH RHYTHMIC GROOVE. ALSO, FOR JACK DEJOHNETTE'S INCREDIBLY MUSICAL YET FIERY SOLO.

BEBOP, FAST SWING, ABAB FORM.

FOUR

SONNY ROLLINS, THE COMPLETE RCA VICTOR RECORDINGS, BMG, 1972.

- MILES DAVIS

FOUR ON SIX

- JOHN L. (WES) MONTGOMERY

DOUBLE PEDAL (TONIC AND DOMINANT) AND BASS OSTINATO.
FREE FALLIN'
(MED.)
TOM PETTY AND THE HEARTBREAKERS, FULL MOON FEVER, UMG RECORDINGS, 1989.
- TOM PETTY/JEFF LYNNE
INTRO
*F Bbsus2 F Csus4 F Bbsus2 F Csus4
*MUSIC REFLECTS SOUNDING KEY (GUITAR CAPO I IN E.)
VERSE
F Bbsus2 F Csus4 F Bbsus2
F Csus4 F Bbsus2 F Csus4
F Bbsus2 F Csus4 F Bbsus2
F Csus4
VERSE
F Bbsus2 F Csus4
F Bbsus2 F Csus4 F Bbsus2
F Csus4 F Bbsus2 F Csus4
TO

CHORUS
F Bbsus2 F Csus4 F Bbsus2
F Csus4 F Bbsus2 F Csus4
F Bbsus2 1. F Csus4 2. F Csus4
INTERLUDE
F Bbsus2
F Csus4 F Bbsus2 1. F Csus4
2. F Csus4
D.S. AL
CHORUS
F Bbsus2 F Csus4
F5 Bbsus2 1. F Csus4 2. F Csus4
INTERLUDE
F5 Bb5 F5 C5 F5 Bb5 F5 C5
OUTRO - CHORUS
F Bbsus2 F Csus4 F Bbsus2 F Csus4
F Bbsus2 F Csus4 F Bbsus2 F Csus4

INNOVATIVE 12-TONE MELODY.

FREEDOM JAZZ DANCE

THE IN SOUND, ATLANTIC RECORDS INC., 1965.

MED. (FUNK ROCK)

- EDDIE HARRIS

N.C. Bb7#11

N.C. Bb7

N.C. Bb7#9

1. 2.

REPEAT HEAD IN/OUT
OPEN SOLOS OVER Bb7

CLASSIC JAZZ BLUES.

FREIGHT TRANE

KENNY BURRELL AND JOHN COLTRANE, KENNY BURRELL & JOHN COLTRANE, JVC VICTOR, 1958.

(MED. UP)

- TOMMY FLANAGAN

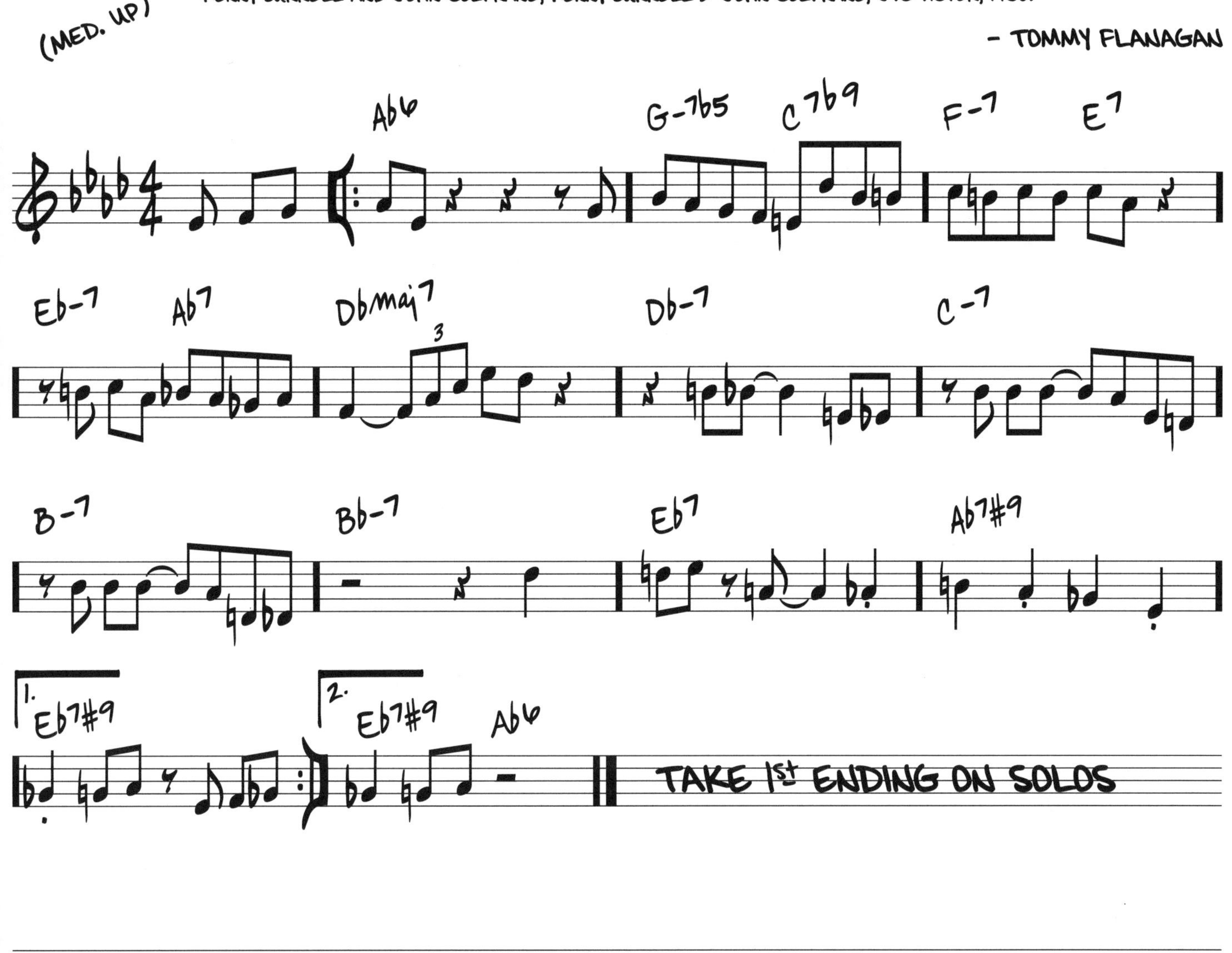

BLUESY SOUNDING MEDIUM-SWING, HARMONICALLY ACCESSIBLE, STANDARD AABA FORM.

GEE BABY, AIN'T I GOOD TO YOU

BILLIE HOLIDAY, BODY AND SOUL, THE VERVE MUSIC GROUP, 1957.

- DON REDMAN/ANDY RAZAF

(MED.)

GENTLE RAIN

- LUIZ BONFA/MATT DUBEY

GET HAPPY

ART TATUM, TEA FOR TWO, X5 MUSIC GROUP, 1945.

- TED KOEHLER/HAROLD ARLEN

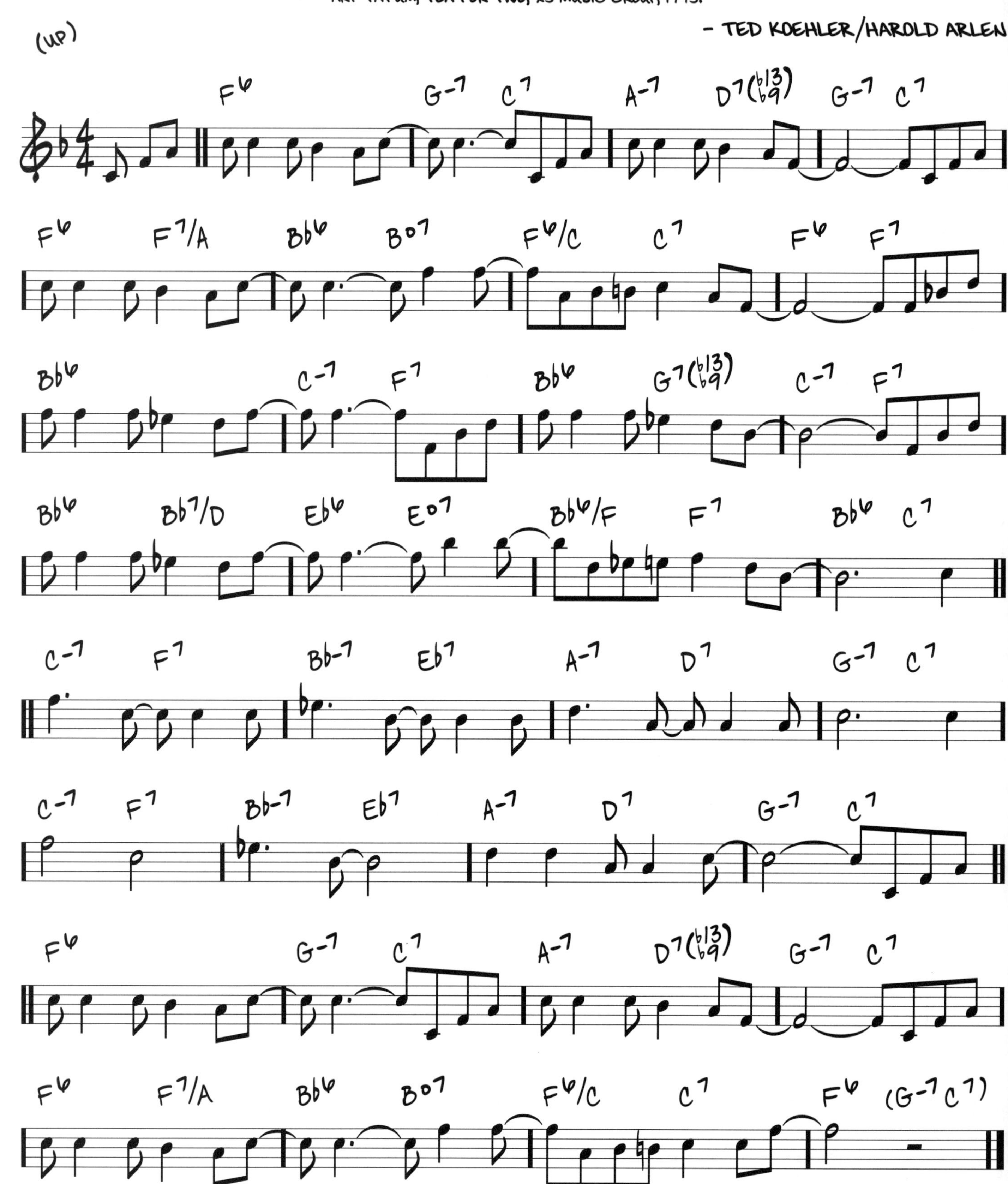

CLASSIC THREE-TONIC TUNE, 16-BAR FORM THAT DIVIDES 9/7, RATHER THAN 8/8. OFTEN PLAYED FAST!

GIANT STEPS

GIANT STEPS, ATLANTIC RECORDING CORPORATION, 1959.

(UP)

- JOHN COLTRANE

Bmaj7 D7 | Gmaj7 Bb7 | Ebmaj7 | A-7 D7 |

Gmaj7 Bb7 | Ebmaj7 F#7 | Bmaj7 | F-7 Bb7 |

Ebmaj7 | A-7 D7 | Gmaj7 | C#-7 F#7 |

Bmaj7 | F-7 Bb7 | Ebmaj7 | C#-7 F#7 ||

FINE

"FLOATING" VERSE BASED ON V (G), WHICH CREATES A G MIXO EFFECT AND RESOLVES EFFECTIVELY INTO C MAJOR CHORUS.

BRIDGE
2.
F C/E F C/E F C/E F C/E C D-/C
E-/C F/C C
D-/C E-/C F/C
TO
*N.C. (G)
*G PEDAL (NEXT 6 MEAS.)
VERSE
N.C. (G)
G C/G G C/G
D.S. AL
(TAKE 2nd ENDING)
G C/G G C/G G C/G
F C/E F C/E F C/G F/A Gsus4/B
OUTRO
C N.C.
REPEAT AND FADE
(GUITAR)

INTRICATE RHYTHMS WITH AN R&B FEEL.

C-7
G-7
F-7
G-7
1. C-7
G-7
2. C-7
G7
F-7
G-7
C-7
G-7
F-7
G-7
C-7
G-7
F-7
G-7
C-7
G-7
F-7
G-7
C-7
G-7
INTERLUDE
F-7
G-7
C-7
G-7
F-7
G-7
1., 2., 3.
C-7
G-7
4.
C-7
OUTRO-CHORUS
F-7
G-7
C-7
G-7
F-7
G-7
C-7
G-7
F-7
G-7
REPEAT AND FADE
C-7
G-7
F-7
G-7
C-7
G-7

BRIDGE HAS NON-FUNCTIONAL HARMONY.

THE GIRL FROM IPANEMA
(GARÔTA DE IPANEMA)

SECONDARY DOMINANTS, MODAL INTERCHANGE, GUIDE TONE LINES, MODULATIONS, EXTENDED SUB V7'S.

GOD BLESS' THE CHILD

BILLIE HOLIDAY, THE COMPLETE BILLIE HOLIDAY, X5 MUSIC GROUP.

- ARTHUR HERZOG JR./BILLIE HOLIDAY

GOLDEN LADY
(MED. ROCK)
- STEVIE WONDER
Ebmaj7 F-7 G-7 A-7 D7sus4
VERSE
Ebmaj7 F-7 G-7 A-7 D7sus4
Ebmaj7 F-7 G-7 A-7 D7sus4
PRE-CHORUS
Ebmaj7 Bbmaj7 Ab-7 Db7 Gbmaj7
F#-7 B7sus4 B7 A-7 D7sus4 *(Eb7b9) TO
CHORUS
*3rd X ONLY
G- G-(maj7) G-7 G-6 Abmaj7
G- G-(maj7) G-7 G-6 Abmaj7
Gmaj7 F-7 Bb7sus4
SOLO
Ebmaj7 F-7 G-7 A-7 D7sus4
LAST X D.S. AL
CHORUS
Ab- Ab-(maj7) Ab-7 Ab-6 Amaj7
A- A-(maj7) A-7 A-6 Bbmaj7
CONT. MODULATING UP 1/2 STEP AFTER EACH REPEATED SECTION AND FADE

GOOD BAIT

(MED. SWING)

- TADD DAMERON/COUNT BASIE

(BALLAD)

GOOD MORNING HEARTACHE

- DAN FISHER/IRENE HIGGINBOTHAM/ERVIN DRAKE

GOODBYE PORK PIE HAT

(BALLAD)

- CHARLES MINGUS

GOT A MATCH?

(FAST SWING)

- CHICK COREA

GRAVY WALTZ

OSCAR PETERSON, EXCLUSIVELY FOR MY FRIENDS: THE LOST TAPES, 1965.

(MED.)

- STEVE ALLEN/RAY BROWN

CLASSIC BEBOP LINES.

GROOVIN' HIGH

KIND OF BLUE, SONY ENTERTAINMENT, 1959.

(BEBOP)

- JOHN "DIZZY" GILLESPIE

Eb6 A-7

D7 Eb6

G-7 C7 F7

1. F-7 Bb7

G-7 F#-7 F-7

Bb7b9 2. F-7 Bb7

F-7 Db7 Eb6 (F-7 Bb7)

FINE

EXAMPLE OF 7TH CHORD INVERSIONS, SECONDARY DOMINANTS, ALTERED DOMINANT CHORD, DECEPTIVE RESOLUTION.

HAUNTED HEART

JANE MONHEIT, IN THE SUN, N-CODED MUSIC, 2002.

(BALLAD)

- HOWARD DIETZ/ARTHUR SCHWARTZ

(MED. UP)
HALF NELSON
- MILES DAVIS
CMaj7
F-7
3
*PLAY CUE ON REPEAT - THEN SOLOS
Bb7
CMaj7
B-7
Bb-7
AbMaj7
A-7
3
D7
D-7
3
G7
E-7
Eb7
AbMaj7
G7
CMaj7
F-7
3
Bb7
CMaj7

B-7
Bb-7
Abmaj7
A-7
D7
D-7
G7
E-7
Eb7
Abmaj7
G7
PLAY HEAD ONCE, THEN SOLOS
AFTER SOLOS, D.C. AL
G7
C maj7

EXAMPLE OF AN ORATORIO.

HALLELUJAH CHORUS

CHICAGO SYMPHONY CHORUS, HANDEL: MESSIAH, DECCA MUSIC GROUP LIMITED, 1985.

(FAST)

– GEORGE FRIDERIC HANDEL

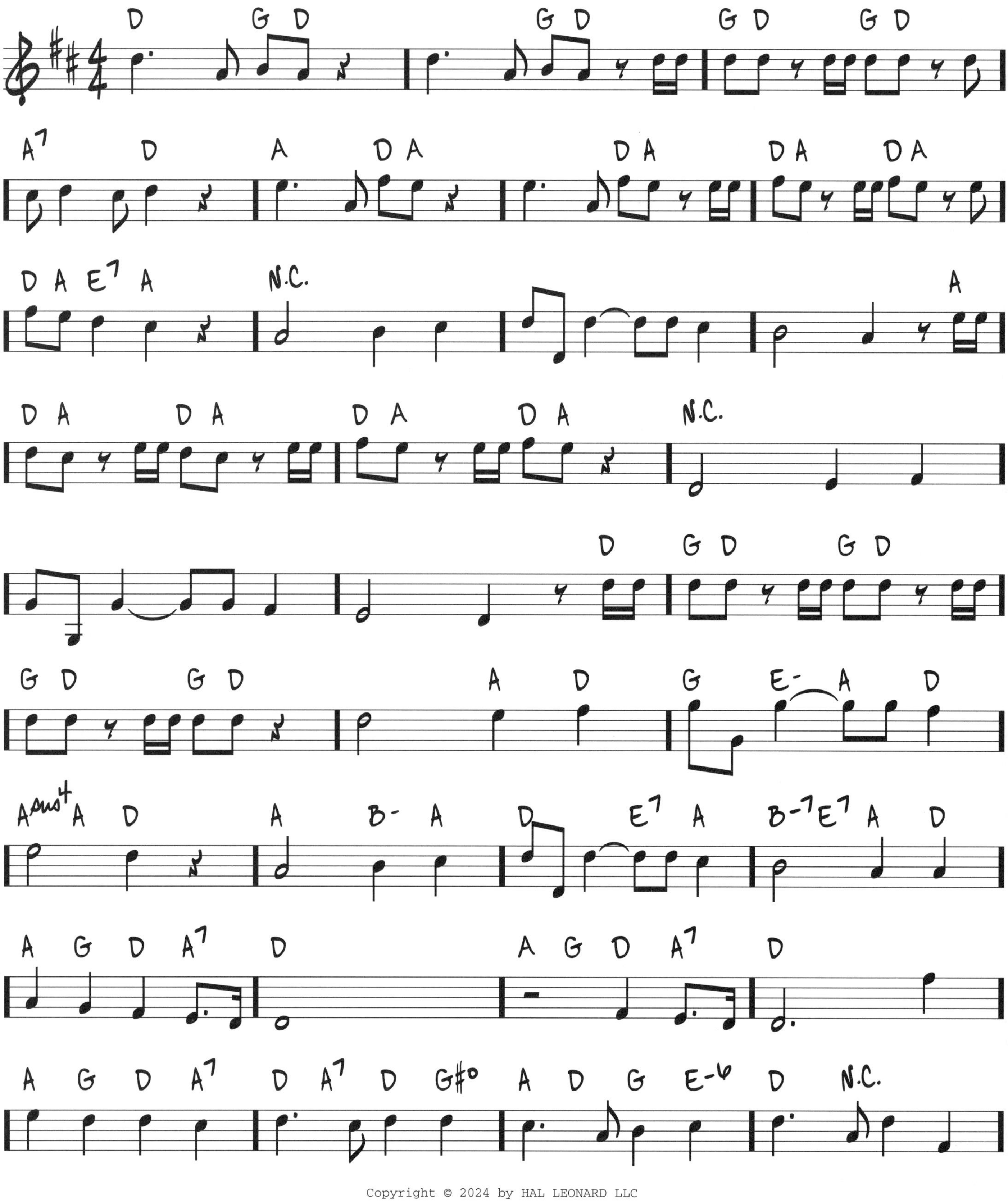

D G D G D G D G D

A7 D A D A D A D A D A

D A E7 A N.C. A

D A D A D A D A N.C.

D G D G D

G D G D A D G E- A D

Asus4 A D A B- A D E7 A B-7 E7 A D

A G D A7 D A G D A7 D

A G D A7 D A7 D G#o A D G E-6 D N.C.

A D G#o A D A E
A A7 D G C#o D G D A D A D
G#o A D A E A N.C. A D A D A D A
D A N.C. A D A D A D A D A N.C.
D G D G D G D G D N.C. E A E
A E A E A E N.C. F# B- F#
B- F# B- F# B- N.C. G
A7 D A B- D G D A7 D Asus4 A
D G D G D G D G D G D
G D G D G D G D

HARD TIMES

RAY CHARLES, PURE GENIUS: THE COMPLETE ATLANTIC RECORDINGS, ATLANTIC RECORDING CORP, 2005.

VERSE

Eb6 F9 E9 | Eb6/9 Ab7

G7 | C- B+

Bb-7 Eb7 G7#5 | Ab6 A°7

Eb7/Bb Ab-6 C7/G | B7#11 Bb7#5

Eb6 Ab9 Gb9 E9 | Eb6/9 Ab7 | G7

C- C-/B | Bb-7 Eb7 G7#5

Ab6 A°7 | Eb7/Bb Ab-6 C7/G

B7#11 Bb7 | Eb6 F9 E9 Eb6/9

MULTITONIC RELATIONSHIPS IN THE BRIDGE. AABA FORM.

HAVE YOU MET MISS JONES?

JOE PASS, VIRTUOSO, FANTASY, INC., 1973.

(MED.)

- LORENZ HART/RICHARD RODGERS

FMAJ7 F#o7 G-7

C7 A-7 D-7

1. G-7 C7 2. C-7 F7

Bbmaj7 Ab-7 Db7 Gbmaj7 E-7 A7

Dmaj7 Ab-7 Db7 Gbmaj7 G-7 C7

Fmaj7 F#o7 G-7 C7 Bb7

A-7 D7 G-7 C7 Fmaj7 (G-7 C7)

GREAT FOR PRACTICING KEEPING A STEADY GROOVE.

HEARTBREAK HOTEL

ELVIS PRESLEY, HOUND DOG MBOPGLOBAL- DELTA, 1968.

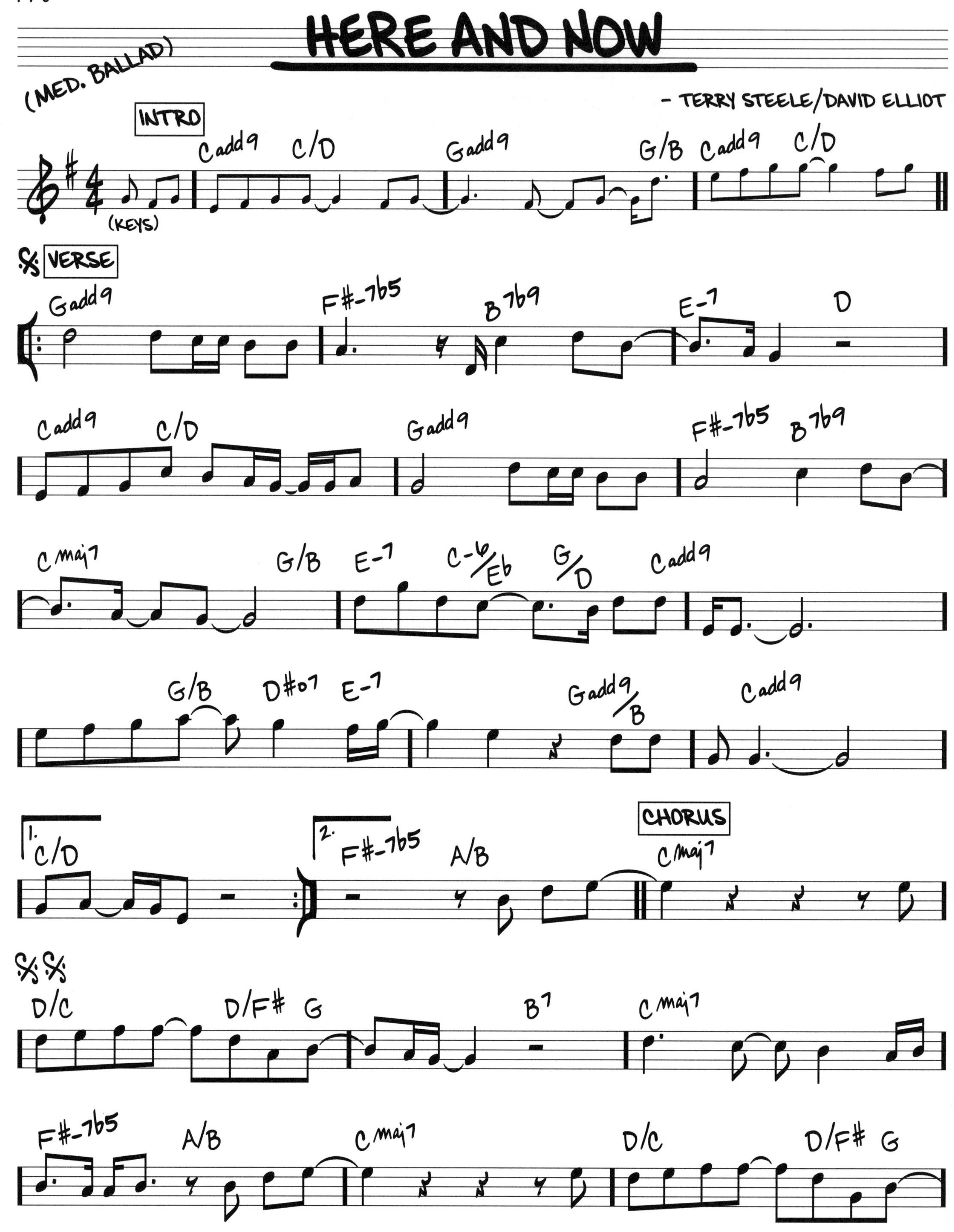
HERE AND NOW
(MED. BALLAD)
- TERRY STEELE/DAVID ELLIOT
INTRO
Cadd9 C/D Gadd9 G/B Cadd9 C/D
(KEYS)
VERSE
Gadd9 F#-7b5 B7b9 E-7 D
Cadd9 C/D Gadd9 F#-7b5 B7b9
Cmaj7 G/B E-7 C-6/Eb G/D Cadd9
G/B D#o7 E-7 Gadd9/B Cadd9
1. C/D
2. F#-7b5 A/B
CHORUS
Cmaj7
D/C D/F# G B7 Cmaj7
F#-7b5 A/B Cmaj7 D/C D/F# G

B7
CMaj7
TO ⊕ 1
TO ⊕ 2
Cadd9
C/D
Gadd9
D.S. AL ⊕ 1
(TAKE 2nd ENDING)
Cadd9
C/D
Gadd9
Cadd9
C/D
⊕ 1
BRIDGE
Cadd9
C/D
E-7
D
GMaj9
E-7
C/D
CHORUS
F/G
G/B
CMaj7
D.S.S. AL ⊕ 2
⊕ 2
OUTRO (W/VOC. AD LIB.)
Cadd9
C/D
Gadd9
G/B
CMaj7
1., 2.
Bbadd9
C
FMaj7
3.
BbMaj9
Cadd9
Gadd9
RIT.

AEOLIAN MODE, WITH INTERESTING MELODY/HARMONY RELATIONSHIPS AND BEAUTIFUL PROSODY.

1.
Asus4
A
2., 3.
Asus4
A
G
G maj7
D
D maj7
B-
Asus4
A
E-(add9)
(PNO. 8VB)
TO ⊕
F♯-
D.S. AL ⊕
⊕
F♯-

ABAC FORM, INTERESTING HARMONIC MOVES, CHALLENGING HARMONY BUT NOT TOO DIFFICULT.

HERE'S THAT RAINY DAY

BILL EVANS, BILL EVANS ALONE, VERVE, 1990 (1968).

(MED.)

- JOHNNY BURKE/JIMMY VAN HEUSEN

HOUSE OF JADE

WAYNE SHORTER, JUJU, BLUE NOTE RECORDS, 1999.

(SLOW SWING)

- WAYNE SHORTER

D-7b5 Dbmaj7 C-7 Db7#11 Eb7 F7 Db7 C7

D-7b5 Dbmaj7 C-7 F7 Eb7 F7 Db7 C-7

Bb-9/Eb

A-9/D D7 E-7 Eb7#11

GOOD JAM-BAND TUNE, EXAMPLE OF NEW ORLEANS FUNK.

HEY POCKY WAY

(MED. FUNK)

THE METERS, REJUVENATION, ATLANTIC RECORDING CORP., 1974.

- LEO NOCENTELLI/GEORGE PORTER/
JOSEPH MODELISTE/ARTHUR NEVILLE

D C G
D C G
D C G
D C G
TO
INTERLUDE
N.C.
(DRUMS)
PLAY 3X
B-
G
D7
(HORNS)
D.S. AL
(NO REPEAT)
OUTRO
D7
REPEAT AND FADE

GOOD JAM-BAND BLUES TUNE.

HIDE AWAY

FREDDY KING, LET'S HIDE AWAY AND DANCE AWAY, GUSTO RECORDS, INC. BLUES, 1991 (1964).

- FREDDIE KING/SONNY THOMPSON

(MED. SHUFFLE)

A E7 A7 E7 B7 TO ⊕ A7 E7 1. B7 2. B7 B E7 A7 E7 B7 E7 C E7 A7 E7 B7 A7 E7 B7

D
E9
N.C.
E9
N.C.
A7
E7
B7
A7
E7
B7
E
E
A
E7
B
A
E
B7
D.S. AL ⊕
A7
E7
E♭7
E7
EVEN

BLUES BASED SONG WITH CONTRASTING REPETITIVE PROGRESSIONS.

HIGHWAY TO HELL

AC/DC, HIGHWAY TO HELL, SONY, 1979.

- ANGUS YOUNG/MALCOLM YOUNG/RONALD BELFORD SCOTT

A
D/A
1.
A
2.
D
G5/D
D
G5/D
D
G5/D
D
A
D/A
G5 D/F#
G5
D/F#
CHORUS
A
D/A
G5
D/F#
A
D/A
G5
D/F#
A
D/A
G5
D/F#
A
N.C.
G5
D
A
D/A
G5
D/F#
A
D/A
OUTRO
FREE TIME
D/A
A5
* STRUM AS FAST AS POSSIBLE

HOUND DOG

- JERRY LEIBER/MIKE STOLLER

Eb7
Bb7
Eb7
CHORUS
Eb7
Ab7
Eb7
3
Bb7
Eb7
FINE
SOLO
12-BAR BLUES IN Eb
W/LEAD VOC. AD LIB.
OPEN
11
LAST X
D.S. AL FINE

CLASSIC ABAA FORM, WITH CHANGES USED IN TUNES SUCH AS "ORNITHOLOGY."

HOW HIGH THE MOON

ELLA FITZGERALD, PURE ELLA, THE VERVE MUSIC GROUP, 1950.

I CAN'T GET STARTED

CARMEN MCRAE, BY SPECIAL REQUEST, GRP RECORDS, 1955.

- IRA GERSHWIN/VERNON DUKE

(SLOW)

FMaj7 D-7 | G-7 C7 | A7 D-7 |
G7 C7sus4 | FMaj7 D-7 | G-7 C7b9 |
1. Eb7b5 D7 | G7 C7sus4 | 2. F6 Eb7 | FMaj7 ||
A-7 D7 | A-7 D7 | GMaj7 CMaj7 | GMaj7 |
G-7 C7 | G-7 C7 | A-7 D7 | G7 C7sus4 ||
FMaj7 D-7 | G-7 C7 | A7 D-7 | G7 C7sus4 |
FMaj7 D7#5 | G-7 C7 | F6 (D7#5 | G-7 C7) ||

FINE

AFTER SOLOS, D.S. AL FINE
(PLAY PICKUPS & TAKE REPEAT)

EXCELLENT LOOK AT ASYMMETRIC FORM.
HUMPTY DUMPTY
CHICK COREA'S AKOUSTIC BAND, ALIVE, UMG RECORDINGS, INC., 1991.
(FAST SWING)
- CHICK COREA
Ebmaj7
Dmaj7
Gbmaj7
Fmaj7
A7#5
Bbmaj7
Bb-7
(Bb-7)
N.C.
D-7
B-7
Ab-7
F-7
Ab-7
TO
Gbmaj7
Bb-7
NO ANTICIPATIONS ON SOLOS
AFTER SOLOS, D.C. AL
Gbmaj7
Emaj7
D7
Db-7
Gb7
Bmaj7
Bb7
Eb-7
C-7
A-7

A CHALLENGING FORM TO HOLD TOGETHER.
WE COMPARE THESE TWO RECORDINGS.

HUMPTY DUMPTY

THIS IS OUR MUSIC, ATLANTIC RECORDING CORPORATION, 1960.
PAT METHENY WITH CHARLIE HADEN AND BILLY HIGGINS, REJOICING, ECM RECORDS, 1983.

- ORNETTE COLEMAN

GOOD FOR DEVELOPING A SENSE OF SWING AND SWING EMBELLISHMENT.

I CAN'T GIVE YOU ANYTHING BUT LOVE

RED GARLAND, RED GARLAND'S PIANO, PRESTIGE, 1956.

- JIMMY MCHUGH/DOROTHY FIELDS

(UP)

I GOT A WOMAN

- RAY CHARLES/RENALD J. RICHARD

DIATONIC HARMONY, INVERSIONS, HYBRID VOICING.

I CAN'T MAKE YOU LOVE ME

F/A
G-7
C-7
Bb/F
F
TO ⊕ INTERLUDE
Eb
Bbadd9
Ebmaj7
Eb
G-11
Eb
Bbadd9/D
C-11
Eb
G-7
Eb
Bb/D
G-7
C-7
Eb
G-7
Eb
Bb/D
G-7
C-7
Bb/F
F
Bb/D
D.S. AL ⊕
⊕ OUTRO
Eb
G-7
Ebmaj7
Bb/D
G-7
C-7
Eb
G-7
Ebmaj7
Bb/D
1., 2.
C-7
3.
Eb
Eb/Bb
Abmaj7

GREAT HORN LINES, TAG ENDING.
I GOT YOU
(I FEEL GOOD)
(MED. FUNK)
JAMES BROWN, MAKE IT FUNKY: 1971-1975, UNIVERSAL RECORDS, 2018 (1996).
- JAMES BROWN
VERSE
D7
G7
D7
A7
G7
TO
1.
N.C.(D9)
2.
N.C.(D9)
INTERLUDE
N.C.(D9)
BRIDGE
G7

D7
G7
VERSE
A7 N.C.
D7
G7
D7
A7
G7
1. N.C.(D9)
(HORNS)
2. N.C.(D9)
D.S. AL ⊕
⊕ N.C.(D9)
OUTRO
A7
G7
N.C.(D9)
A7
G7
N.C.(D9)
RIT.
D9

SWINGING JAZZ TUNE WITH GREAT HARMONY AND HARMONIC MOTION.

I HEAR A RHAPSODY

JOHN COLTRANE, LUSH LIFE, CONCORD MUSIC GROUP, INC., 1957.
-KEITH JARRETT, TRIBUTE, ECM 1990.

- GEORGE FRAJOS/JACK BAKER/DICK GASPARRE

INTERESTING HARMONICALLY, RICH MELODY, AABA' FORM, STARTS WITH DESCENDING MAJOR 7 LEAP.

DIATONIC, WITH A LINE CLICHÉ
I JUST CALLED TO SAY I LOVE YOU
THE WOMAN IN RED (MUSIC FROM THE MOTION PICTURE SOUNDTRACK), UMG, 1984.
(MED.)
- STEVIE WONDER
INTRO
Db
N.C.
VERSE
Db
Eb-
Eb-(maj7)
Eb-
Eb-(maj7)
Eb-7
Eb-(maj7)
1., 3.
Eb-
Ab7sus4
Ab
Db
N.C.
2., 4.
Ab7sus4
Ab
Db
TO
N.C.
CHORUS
Eb-7
Ab
Db
Eb-7
Ab
Bb-
Eb-7
Ab
Bb-
D.S. AL
(TAKE REPEAT
Eb-7
Ab7sus4
Ab7
Db
N.C.

CHORUS

(Db) D | E-7 A | D

E-7 A | B-

E-7 A | B-

E-7 A7sus4 A7 | D

CHORUS

(D) Eb | F-7 Bb | Eb

F-7 Bb | C-

F-7 Bb | C-

F-7 Bb7sus4 Bb7 | Eb

B Db | Eb | N.C.

R&B BALLAD FEATURING CHARACTERISTIC HARMONIC AND RHYTHMIC DEVICES.

I MISS YOU

THE TRUTH, UMG RECORDINGS, INC., 1993.

(SLOW)

- AARON HALL/KENNY BURRELL/GREGORY CAUTHEN

CHORUS

N.C. (KEYBOARD) Ab-11 Gbadd9/Bb Cbmaj7 *(Eb-7) Cb6 *2nd X

1. Gbsus2/Bb Eb-7 2. Bb-7 Eb-7 Ab-7 Db Db/F

VERSE

Gbadd9 Cbmaj7

Bb-7 Eb-7 Ab-7

Cb/Db Db/F Gb C-7b5 Cbmaj7

Bb-7 Eb-7 Ab-7

F-7b5 Bb7b9 Bb7

PRE-CHORUS

Eb-7 Bb/D

Gb/Db C-7b5 Cbmaj7 Bb-7 Eb-7 Ab-7 Bb-7 Db/Eb

CHORUS
Ab-11
Gbadd9/Bb
Cbmaj7
Cb6
Gbsus2/Bb
Eb-7
Ab-11
Gbsus2/Bb
Cbmaj7
Eb-7
1.
Bb-7
Eb-7
Ab-7
Db
Db/F
2.
Bb-7
Db/Eb
Gb
BRIDGE
Ab-7
Fbmaj7
Db-9
Gb13
Db-9
Gb13
Eb7(b13 #9)
Ab-7
Fbmaj7
Db-9
Eb-9
Ab13
Db-9
Eb-9
Eb7#9
OUTRO-CHORUS
Ab-11
Gbsus2/Bb
Cbmaj7
Cb6
Bb-7
Eb-7
PLAY 5X
Ab-11
Gbsus2/Bb
Absus2/C
Bbsus2/D
Eb-7
Db/F
Gb
REPEAT AND FADE
Ab-11
Gbsus2/Bb
Cbmaj7
Cb6
Bb-7
Eb-7

I PUT A SPELL ON YOU

- JAY HAWKINS

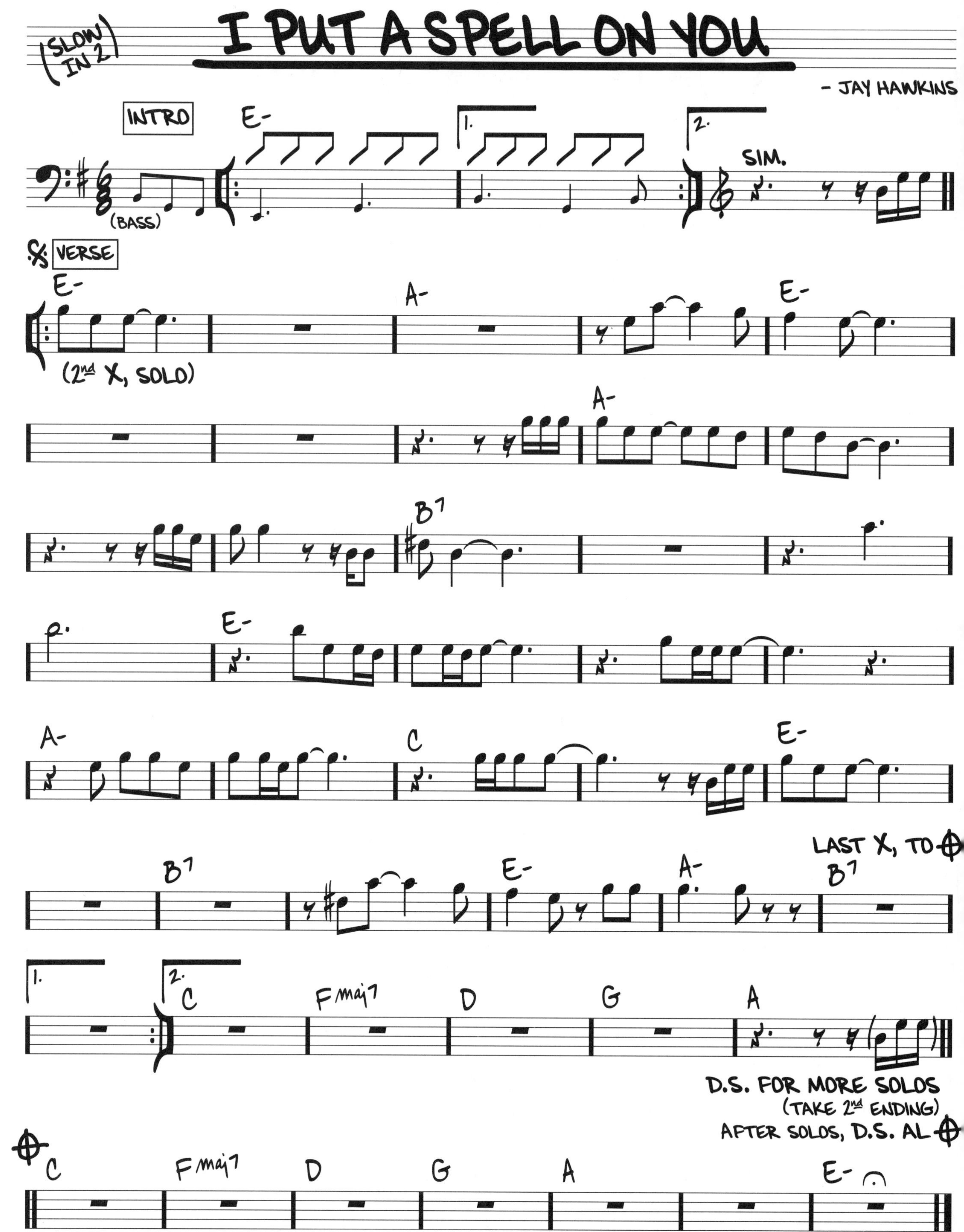

BASED ON CHORD PROGRESSIONS FROM THE JAZZ STANDARDS REPERTOIRE.

I REMEMBER YOU

JIMMY DORSEY, I REMEMBER YOU, EMPIRE, 1995.

- JOHNNY MERCER/VICTOR SCHERTZINGER

EXAMPLE OF SIMILE, ABBA RHYME SCHEME, AND VARYING THE NUMBER OF LINES TO CREATE TENSION.

I REMEMBER THAT

STEPHEN SONDHEIM, SONDHEIM SINGS, BPS CLASSICS, 2005.

- STEPHEN SONDHEIM

G7
C6
E-7
E+ A-7
F#-7
B7
BRIDGE
Emaj7
E6
F#-7b5
B7
Emaj7
A-7
D7
D-7
G7
VERSE
C6
A-
A-(maj7)
A-7
A-6
D-9/A
D-7b5
C6
A-7
D7
A-7
D7
A-7
D7
A-7
Ab7
G7sus4
G7
1. C6
2. C6

ONE OF MANY JAZZ STANDARDS FAMOUSLY REHARMONIZED BY BILL EVANS.

I SHOULD CARE

THELONIOUS MONK, SOLO MONK, SONY MUSIC ENTERTAINMENT INC., 1964.

- SAMMY CAHN/PAUL WESTON/AXEL STORDAHL

(BALLAD)

E-7 A7 F#-7 B7 E-7 A7 Dmaj7

F#-7b5 B7 E-7 G-7 C7

Dmaj7 C#-7b5 F#7 A-7 D7 Gmaj7

C#-7b5 F#7b9 B-7 E7 E-7 A7

E-7 A7 F#-7 B7 E-7 A7 Dmaj7

F#-7b5 B7 E-7 G-7 C7

Dmaj7 C#-7b5 F#7 B-7 E7

E-7 A7 D6 (Gmaj7 F#-7 B7)

MODAL INTERCHANGE, SECONDARY DOMINANTS, MODULATION, CONSTANT STRUCTURE, RHYTHMICIZED DOMINANT PEDAL, DECEPTIVE RESOLUTION.

I'LL BE AROUND

A-7
D7#9
G-7
C7b9sus4
Dbmaj7
C-7
Bb-11
Ab9sus4
Gbmaj7#11
Fmaj7
D-7
C
C#-7
F#7
C-7
F7
B-7
C-7
Gb7
F7
Bbmaj7
D7#9
F#-7
Bb7/F
E-7b5
A7#9
D-
D-7
D-6
C7sus4
A13b9
Bb-6
D
A-7
D-7
Bbmaj7
A7#9
D-7
C-7
B-7b5
E7#9
RIT. LAST X
A7#9
D7#9
G-7
C7b9sus4
TO

Fmaj7
Bbmaj7
Dbmaj7
Ebadd9
(SYNTH.)
C PEDAL
Dbmaj7#5
Bbmaj7
Dbmaj7/Eb
F7
(C PEDAL)
E
SOLO
B-7
E7
C-7
F7
C#-7
D-7
Ab7
G7
Cmaj7
B-7b5
E7
A-7
G7
C7
F#-7
B7
F
E-
E-7
A7
D-7
D.S. AL
G7
C13sus4
B/C
C13sus4
Gb(addb9)/Bb
Dbmaj7#5
Bbmaj7
Dbmaj7
Ebadd9
(SYNTH.)
C PEDAL
A TEMPO
Dbmaj7#5
Bbmaj7
Dbmaj7
E7#9
(C PEDAL)
REPEAT AND FADE

MOSTLY DIATONIC, E CHORDS, MODAL INTERCHANGE.
I TRY TO THINK ABOUT ELVIS
PATTY LOVELESS, WHEN FALLEN ANGELS FLY, SONY BMG MUSIC ENTERTAINMENT, 1994.
(MED.)
- GARY BURR
INTRO
E
BAND TACET
DRUMS ENTER
(GUITAR)
VERSE
E 1st X, BASS TACET
A
E
C#-
B
A
B
E
1.
N.C.
2.
BRIDGE
C#-
F#
A
E
C#-
F#
A

B
TO ⊕
SOLO
D
E
A
B
E
D.S. AL ⊕
⊕
N.C.
VERSE
F♯
B
F♯
E
F♯
D♯-
C♯
F♯
B
C♯
D♯-
G♯
B
C♯
F♯
OUTRO
F♯ N.C.
F♯
(GUITAR)

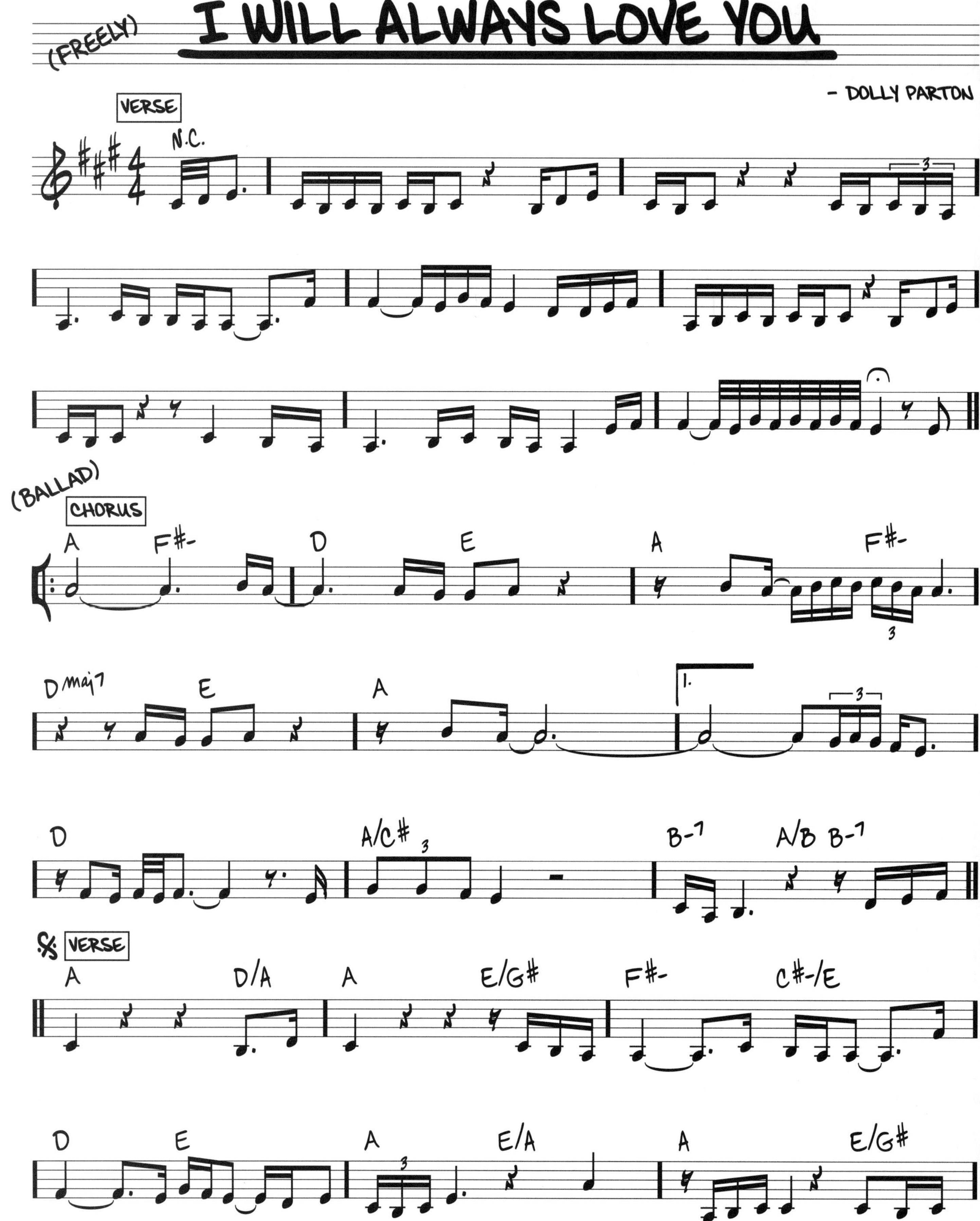
(FREELY)
I WILL ALWAYS LOVE YOU
- DOLLY PARTON
VERSE
N.C.
(BALLAD)
CHORUS
A F#- D E A F#-
Dmaj7 E A 1.
D A/C# B-7 A/B B-7
VERSE
A D/A A E/G# F#- C#-/E
D E A E/A A E/G#

TO
2.
F#-
C#-/E
D maj7
E
C#-/E
C-/E
B-/E
SAX SOLO
A
D/A
A
E/G#
F#-
C#-/E
D
E
A
E/A
A
C#-
F#-
C#-/E
D maj7
E
D.S. AL
CHORUS
B
G#-
E maj7
F#
B
G#-
C#-7
F#
B
G#-
E maj7
F#
B
G#-
C#-7
F#
B
G#-
3
E maj7
F#
B
G#-
(FREELY)
E maj7
F#
N.C.
E
RIT.
B/D#
E/F#
Badd9

I WISH
STEVIE WONDER, SONGS IN THE KEY OF LIFE, SONY, 1976.
- STEVIE WONDER
(MED. FUNK)
INTRO
N.C.
(BASS)
Eb-7
Ab7
VERSE
Bb7
C7
F-7
Ab-6
5
Bb7#5

Eb-7
Ab7
Bb7
C7
F-7
Ab-6
5
CHORUS
Bb7#5
TO
D.S. AL
OUTRO
(BASS)
REPEAT AND FADE
(HORNS)

CLASSIC MOTOWN BALLAD FROM EARLY IN THE KING OF POP'S CAREER.

I'LL BE THERE

JACKSON 5, JACKSON 5: THE ULTIMATE COLLECTION, UMG RECORDINGS, 2000.

- BERRY GORDY JR./HAL DAVIS/WILLIE HUTCH/BOB WEST

(MED.)

INTRO

VERSE

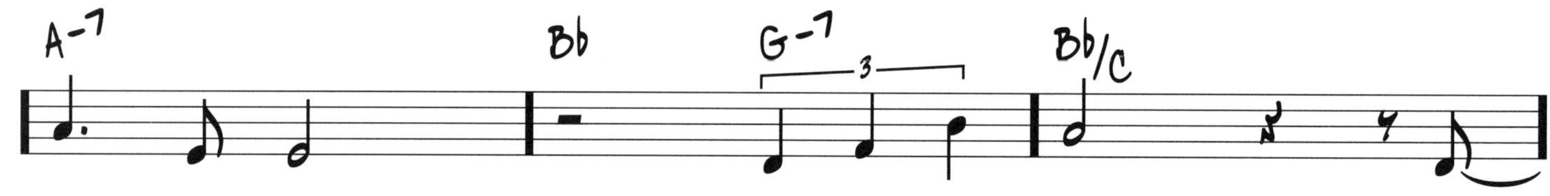

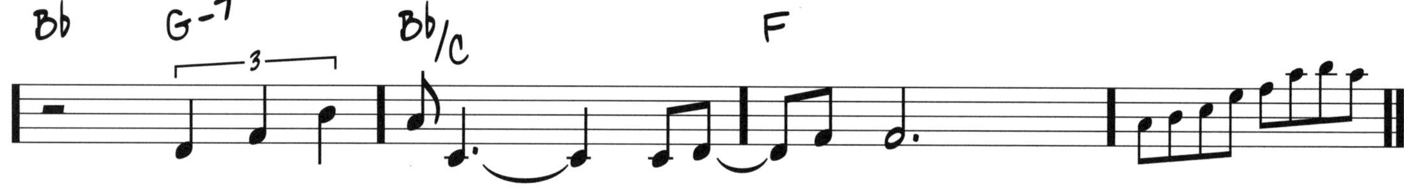

BRIDGE
Ab
Eb
Bb
F
Ab
Eb
Bb
F
Fsus4
VERSE
F
C/E
D-7
F/C
A-7
Bb
G-7
3
Bb/C
F
OUTRO-CHORUS
F
C/E
D-7
F/C
A-7
Bb
G-7
3
Bb/C
F
REPEAT AND FADE

EXAMPLE OF TTBB ARRANGEMENT.

I'LL NEVER FALL IN LOVE AGAIN

BURT BACHARACH, MAKE IT EASY ON YOURSELF, UMG RECORDINGS, INC., 1969.

(MED.)

- HAL DAVID/BURT BACHARACH

INTRO

D G maj7 D G maj7

(TRUMPET)

D D maj7 D D maj7

VERSE

D B-7

G maj7 F♯-7

B7 sus4 B7 E-7 A7

G7 D G

A D D maj7 1. D D maj7

2. D

BRIDGE

*G/A D G/A

*2nd X, TRUMPET PLAYS MELODY, 1st 4 MEAS.

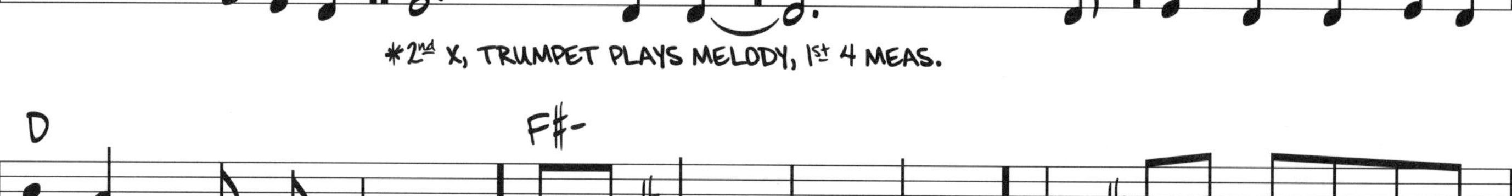

E7
A
VERSE
D
B-7
Gmaj7
F#-7
B7sus4
B7
E-7
A7
G7
TO ⊕
D
G
A
D
Dmaj7
D
D.S. AL ⊕
(TRUMPET)
⊕
D
E-7
A7
G7
D
FREELY
G
A
OUTRO
A TEMPO
D
Gmaj7
D
Gmaj7
D
Dmaj7
D
REPEAT AND FADE
Dmaj7

I'M OLD FASHIONED
(BALLAD OR MED. SWING)
JOHN COLTRANE, BLUE TRAIN, BLUE NOTE RECORDS, 1957.
- JOHNNY MERCER/JEROME KERN
F6 D-7 G-7 C7 Fmaj7 D-7 G-7 C7
Eo7/F Fmaj7 E-7b5 A7b9
D-7 G7 D-7 G7
G-7 Bb6 Bo7 C7sus4 C7
F6 D-7 G-7 C7 Fmaj7 D-7 B-7 E7
Amaj7 B-7 C#-7 Dmaj7 E7 F#o7 G-7 C7
F6 D-7 G-7 C7 Fmaj7 D-7 G-7 C7
C-7 F7 Bbmaj7 Eb7 A-7 D-7 B-7b5 Bb-6
A-7 D-7 G-7 C7 F6 (D-7 G-7 C7)

MINOR PENTATONIC MELODY, EXPANDED BLUES FORM, STOP TIME.

I'M YOUR HOOCHIE COOCHIE MAN

MUDDY WATERS, THE CHESS 50TH ANNIVERSARY COLLECTION: MUDDY WATERS—HIS BEST 1947 TO 1955, UMG RECORDINGS, 1997.

- WILLIE DIXON

(SLOW SHUFFLE)

INTRO

A7 N.C. A7 N.C. A7

VERSE W/INTRO RIFF

A7 N.C. A7 N.C. A7

N.C. A7 N.C. A7

N.C. A7 N.C. A7

N.C. A7

CHORUS

D7 A7

E7 D7

1., 2. A A7/C# D7 Eb°7 A E7

3. A A7/C# D7 Eb°7 A/E Ab7 A7

MELODIC STEP PROGRESSION IN THE CHORUS AND INTERESTING MELODY/HARMONY RELATIONSHIPS THOUGHOUT.

I'M WITH YOU

AVRIL LAVIGNE, LET GO, ARISTA RECORDS INC., 2002.

- AVRIL LAVIGNE/LAUREN CHRISTY/SCOTT SPOCK/GRAHAM EDWARDS

BRIDGE
E5
B-7
E
B-7
E
D
C#-
E
OUTRO-CHORUS
A5
B5
D5
A5
B5
D5
A5
B5
D5
F#-
E/G#
D
A
Bsus4
D
A
B
D
A
Bsus4
D
F#-
E
1.
D
2.
D
F#5
D5
F#5
D5
A5

INTERESTING KEY RELATIONSHIP AT THE BRIDGE; GOOD FOR DEVELOPING A SENSE OF SWING.

I'VE GOT THE WORLD ON A STRING

FRANK SINATRA, FRANK SINATRA 80TH: ALL THE BEST, CAPITOL RECORDS, 1995.

- TED KOEHLER/HAROLD ARLEN

BASED ON CHORD PROGRESSIONS FROM THE JAZZ STANDARDS REPERTOIRE.

(MED.)

IF I SHOULD LOSE YOU

NINA SIMONE, WILD IS THE WIND, THE VERVE MUSIC GROUP, 1966.

- LEO ROBIN/RALPH RAINGER

STRAIGHT-EIGHTH MODAL TUNE WITH LONG MELODY NOTES AND A LOT OF SPACE.
ICARUS
(EVEN 8ths)
RALPH N. TOWNER, DIARY, ECM RECORDS, 1973.
- RALPH N. TOWNER
Gadd9
D-7/G
1.
C-9/G
2.
Gadd9
G7sus4
G7
Cmaj7#11
Fmaj9
Dadd9
FINE

B-9/F#
G7sus4
B-9/F#
D-7/G
Cadd9
G-9/C
G-9/Bb
Ebmaj7#11
Fmaj7/G
(OPTIONAL REPEAT)
SOLO ON ENTIRE FORM
AFTER SOLOS, D.S. AL FINE
(PLAY PICKUP)

USED TO PRACTICE TRANSCRIPTION.

IF I AIN'T GOT YOU

(MED. BALLAD)

ALICIA KEYS, THE DIARY OF ALICIA KEYS, BJ RECORDS, 2003.

- ALICIA AUGELLO COOK

B-7
A-7
G maj7
A-7
B-7
CHORUS
C maj7
B-7
A-7
G maj7
A-7
B-7
C maj7
B-7
Bb-7
A-7
TO
G maj7
G maj7
D.S. AL
D/A
G/B
OUTRO W/INTRO RIFF
G maj7
N.C.
C maj7
B-7
A-7
G maj7
A-7
B-7
C maj7
B-7
A-7
G maj7
RIT.
FREELY
8VA
(PIANO)
15VB

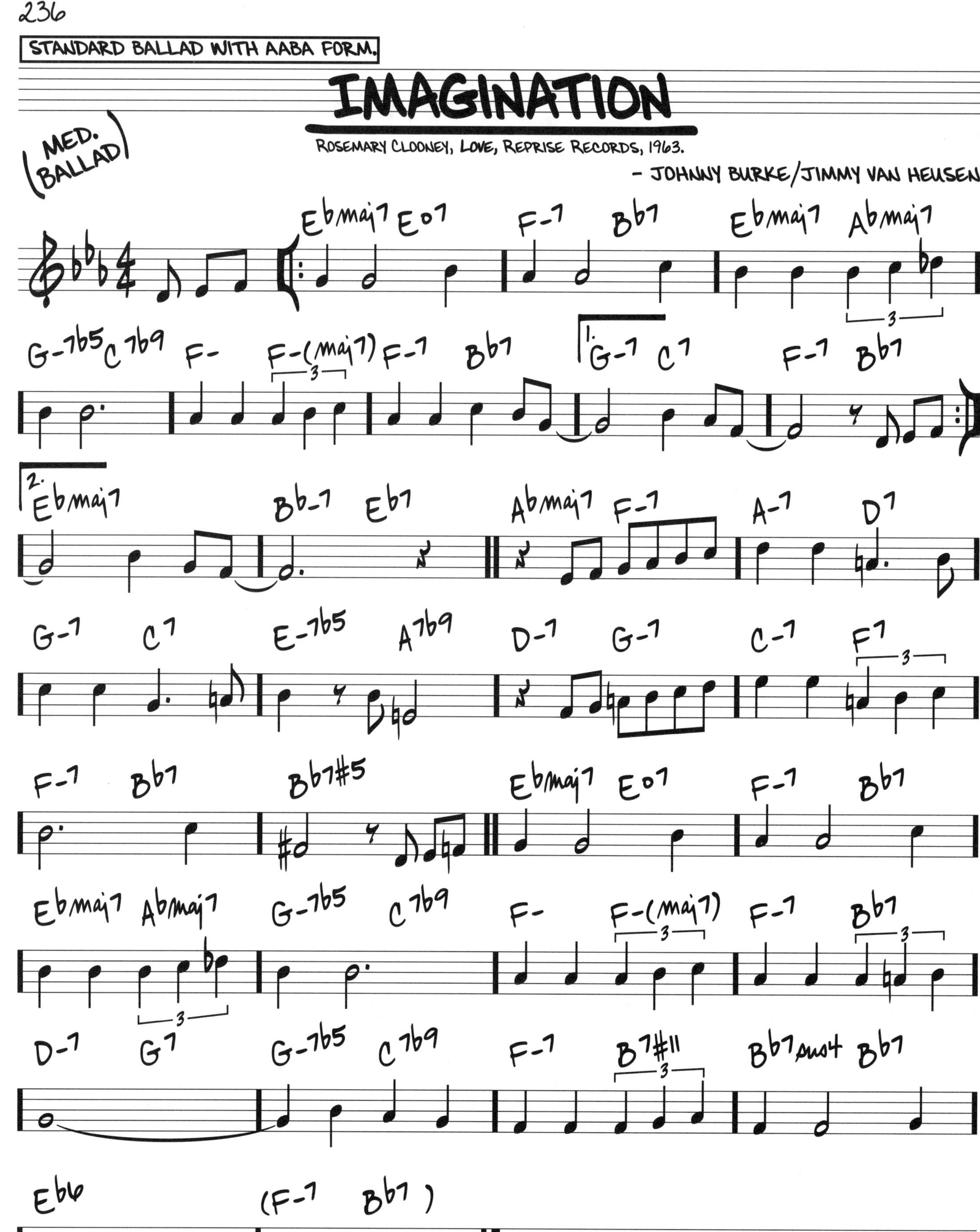
STANDARD BALLAD WITH AABA FORM.
IMAGINATION
ROSEMARY CLOONEY, LOVE, REPRISE RECORDS, 1963.
MED. BALLAD
- JOHNNY BURKE/JIMMY VAN HEUSEN
Ebmaj7 Eo7 F-7 Bb7 Ebmaj7 Abmaj7
G-7b5 C7b9 F- F-(maj7) F-7 Bb7 G-7 C7 F-7 Bb7
Ebmaj7 Bb-7 Eb7 Abmaj7 F-7 A-7 D7
G-7 C7 E-7b5 A7b9 D-7 G-7 C-7 F7
F-7 Bb7 Bb7#5 Ebmaj7 Eo7 F-7 Bb7
Ebmaj7 Abmaj7 G-7b5 C7b9 F- F-(maj7) F-7 Bb7
D-7 G7 G-7b5 C7b9 F-7 B7#11 Bb7sus4 Bb7
Eb6 (F-7 Bb7)

MODAL TUNE, AABA FORM, OFTEN PLAYED FAST, GOOD FOR MODAL IMPROVISATION.

IMPRESSIONS

HERBIE HANOCK, DIRECTION IN MUSIC: CELEBRATING MILES DAVIS AND JOHN COLTRANE, THE VERVE MUSIC GROUP, 2002.

- JOHN COLTRANE

AN EXCELLENT ILLUSTRATION OF BRUSHES BEING UTILIZED IN A CONTEMPORARY GOSPEL SETTING.
IMAGINE ME
(MED. SLOW)
KIRK FRANKLIN, HERO, BZOMBA GOSPEL LLC, 2005.
- KIRK FRANKLIN
INTRO
(KEYBOARD)
VERSE
CONT. SIM.
PRE-CHORUS
1.
2, 3.
Fsus2
C/E
G/B
C
A-7

CHORUS

D- C/E F | Fsus2 C/E

G/B Bb/C C7 | Fsus2 C/E

G/B C | Fsus2 C/E

G/B Bb/C C7 | Fsus2 C/E TO 𝄌

G/B C D.S. AL 𝄌 | 𝄌 G/B C

Fsus2 C/E | G/B Bb/C C7

Fsus2 C/E | G/B C

Fsus2 C/E | G/B Bb/C C7

Fsus2 C/E | G/B C

OUTRO

REPEAT AND FADE

Fsus2 C/E | Fsus2 C/E | Fsus2 C/E | G/B C

EXCELLENT MINOR CLICHÉ LINES.

IN A SENTIMENTAL MOOD

DUKE ELLINGTON & JOHN COLTRANE, DUKE ELLINGTON & JOHN COLTRANE, THE VERVE MUSIC GROUP, 1993.

FUNKY SOUL JAM TUNE, HARMONICALLY SIMPLE, WITH GREAT BASS LINE AND GROOVE.

IN FULL SWING

(FUNK)

THE QUIET REVOLUTION, FOURTH AND BROADWAY, 1993.

- MARK O'CONNOR

GREAT HORN LINES.
IN THE MOOD
GLENN MILLER, THE FABULOUS GLENN MILLER AND HIS ORCHESTRA, 1972.
(MED. SWING)
- JOE GARLAND
N.C.
Bb7
Bb9
Eb9
Db6
A
Ab6
Ab7
Db6
Db7
Ab6
Eb7
Ab6
Db6
1.
E7
Bb-7
2.
E7
Eb7sus4
Ab6
B (PLAY 4X)
Ab6
B°7
Bb-7
Eb7
SOLO 3rd AND 4th TIMES
1., 3.
Eb7
Eb°7
E7
PLAY ON SOLO
2., 4.
UNISON

Eb7 E7 Eb7 E7 Eb7 Eb+ Ab6
C SOLO
(SOLO OVER A CHANGES)
9
(Eb7)
Ab6 E7 Eb9 Ab6 N.C. Eb7
(PLAY AS WRITTEN LAST TIME ONLY)
Ab6
Db6 Db7 Ab6
TO
Eb7
N.C.
1., 2.
3.
D.S. AL
CONT. A♭ PEDAL
Ab6
N.C.

CLASSIC R&B, WITH BIG, FUNKY SOUND.
IN THE STONE
(MED. FUNK)
EWF, IN THE STONE, MUSIC ENTERTAINMENT, INC., 1979.
- MAURICE WHITE/DAVID FOSTER/ALLEE WILLIS
INTRO
B add9
B/A
(TRUMPETS)
Gmaj7 E-7
E/F#
E+/F#
E♭/F#
B add9
B/A
2nd X, TRUMPETS TACET
Gmaj7 E-7
E/F#
E+/F#
E♭/F#
VERSE
B add9
B/A
1st X, INSTRUMENTAL
2nd X, VOCAL
Gmaj7 E-7
1., 2.
E/F#
E+/F#
E♭/F#
3.
E/F#
E+/F#
E♭/F#
CHORUS
B
E-7
G/A
C#7sus4
B/F# C#/G# D#/A#

TO ⊕
B
E-7
G/A
F#/G# E/F#
VERSE
B add9
B/A
Gmaj7 E-7
1.
E/F#
E+/F#
E♭/F#
2.
E/F#
D.S. AL ⊕
E+/F#
E♭/F
OUTRO
B B/D# F#- A A# B E A A#
B B/D# F#- A A# B E A A#
B B/D# F#- A A# B E A A#
PLAY 3X
B B/D# F#- A A# B E A A# B
F#- A A# B
1., 2.
E A A#
3.
E A A# B

GREAT RHYTHMIC MELODY AND COUNTER LINES.

IN WALKED BUD

(MED. UP SWING)

THE THELONIOUS MONK QUARTET, MYSTERIOSO, FANTASY, INC., 1958.

- THELONIOUS MONK

F- F-(maj7) F-7 Bb7 Eb7

Ab6 F7 Bb-7 Eb7 Ab6 1. C7(b13 b9) 2. (Ab6)

F- Db7

F- Db7

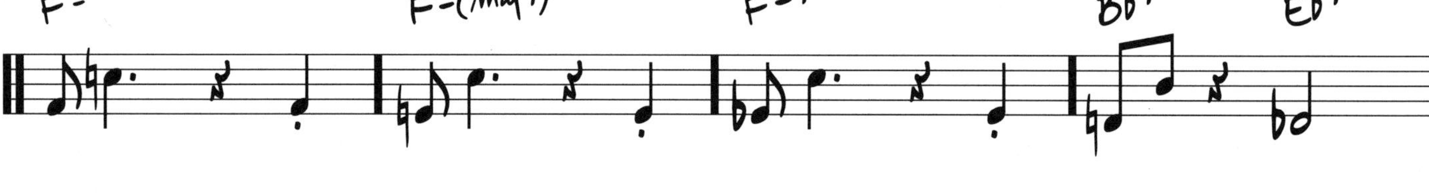

AFTER SOLOS, D.C. AL ⊕
(TAKE REPEAT)

IN YOUR OWN SWEET WAY

GOOD FOR LEARNING TO READ CHORD CHANGES.

INDIANA
(BACK HOME AGAIN IN INDIANA)

(UP SWING)

OSCAR PETERSON TRIO, AT THE CONCERTGEBOUW (LIVE), THE VERVE MUSIC GROUP, 1957.
CLARK TERRY, DIZZY GILLESPIE, AND ROY ELDRIDGE, THE TRUMPET KINGS AT MONTREUX 1975, FANTASY INC., 1975.

AN ASYMMETRICAL BALLAD DEMONSTRATING GREAT JAZZ WRITING MELODICALLY AND HARMONICALLY.

INNER CITY BLUES

(MAKE ME WANNA HOLLER)

(MED. SLOW FUNK)

- MARVIN GAYE/JAMES NYX

INTRO

Eb-7

PLAY 11 X

(CONT. SIM.)

(PIANO)

1.

2.

VERSE

Eb-7

CHORUS

Ab7sus4

Ab7

Ab7sus4

3rd X, TO ⊕ 1

1.
Ab7
Eb-7
2.
TO ⊕ 2
INTERLUDE
Eb-7
1. - 6.
7.
D.S. AL ⊕ 1
⊕ 1
Ab7
D.S. AL ⊕ 2
(TAKE 2nd ENDING)
⊕ 2
OUTRO
Eb-7
REPEAT AND FADE
(W/VOC. AD LIB.)

ALLOWS IMPROVISATION IN LOCRIAN AND LYDIAN MODES.
INNER URGE
JOE HENDERSON, INNER URGE, BLUE NOTE, 1973.
(MED. UP)
- JOE HENDERSON
F#-7b5
Fmaj7b5
Ebmaj7b5
Dbmaj7b5
Emaj7b5
Dbmaj7
Dmaj7
Bmaj7#11
Cmaj7
Amaj7
Bb7
Gmaj7
*( )
REPEAT HEAD IN/OUT
* LAST X

UNUSUAL KEY SHIFTS AND HARMONIC TWISTS, INTERESTING MELODIC ANTICIPATIONS AT TIMES MOVING INDEPENDENTLY OF THE CHORD STRUCTURES.

ISFAHAN

FROM **FAR EAST SUITE**

DUKE ELLINGTON, FAR EAST SUITE, BMG MUSIC, 1967.

(BALLAD)

- DUKE ELLINGTON/ BILLY STRAYHORN

TWO-PART VOCAL HARMONY, MODAL INTERCHANGE.
UNUSUAL BRIDGE. VERSE ALSO CONTAINS A REFRAIN.
IRONIC
(MED. ROCK)
ALANIS MORISSETTE, JAGGED LITTLE PILL, MAVERICKS RECORDING COMPANY, 1995.
- ALANIS MORISSETTE/GLEN BALLARD
INTRO
Emaj7
Badd9/F#
Emaj7
VERSE
F#/A#
Badd9
F#/A#
G#-7
TO 1
PRE-CHORUS
CHORUS
F#
B
G#-

A
E
TO 2
1.
F♯
2.
F♯
BRIDGE
E maj7
B add9/F♯
E maj7
B add9/F♯
E maj7
B add9/F♯
E maj7
D.S. AL 1
1
F♯/A♯
G♯-7
PRE-CHORUS
F♯/A♯
B add9
F♯/A♯
G♯-7
F♯/A♯
B add9
F♯/A♯
G♯-7
D.S.S. AL 2
2
F♯
OUTRO
E maj7
B add9/F♯
E maj7
B add9/F♯
E maj7
B add9/F♯
E maj7

GREAT CHANGES; MELODY IS WITHIN ONE OCTAVE.

ISN'T SHE LOVELY

STEVIE WONDER, SONGS IN THE KEY OF LIFE, UMG RECORDINGS, INC., 1976.

- STEVIE WONDER

BASED ON CHORD PROGRESSIONS FROM THE JAZZ STANDARDS REPERTOIRE.

IT COULD HAPPEN TO YOU

CHET BAKER, IT COULD HAPPEN TO YOU, FANTASY, INC., 1958.

- JOHNNY BURKE/JAMES VAN HEUSEN

CLASSIC AABA FORM, WITH SIMPLE CALYPSO HARMONY AND GREAT FEEL.
JAMENTO
(MED. LATIN EVEN 8ths)
MONTY ALEXANDER 7, JAMENTO, FANTASY, INC., 1978.
- MONTY ALEXANDER
A
C6
A+/C#
D-
G7
C6
A7
D-7
C/G
G7
C6
B
C6
C#o7
D-
G7
C6
A7
D-
C/G
G7
C13
C
F
D/F#
G-7
C7
F
F7
E7
Eb7
D7
G-7
F/C
C7
F
TO
N.C.
D
C
Cmaj7
C#o7
D-7
G7
C
A7
D-7
C/G
G7
C
AFTER SOLOS, D.C. AL
N.C.
E
C6
D-
G7
N.C.
PERC. FILL
(G7)
(C)

DANCING 3/4 TUNE, WITH SCALE PATTERNS AND A MELODY THAT'S FUN TO PLAY.

JESUS CHILDREN OF AMERICA

STEVIE WONDER, INNERVISIONS, 1973.

- STEVIE WONDER

Eb-7
Ab/Eb
VERSE
Db-7
Gb9
Cbmaj7
Bb7#5
CHORUS
Ab9
E/F#
F-11
Bb7#9
1.
2.
OUTRO
REPEAT AND FADE
(KEYBOARD)

BEBOP, MINOR KEY. INTERESTING BRIDGE, FOR ADVANCED IMPROVISATION.
JORDU
FLIGHT TO DENMARK, STEEPLECHASE, 1973.
- DUKE JORDAN
(MED. UP JAZZ)
D.S. FOR SOLOS A A B A
CHANGES ON THE BEAT/COMP. THROUGH BREAKS
AFTER SOLOS, D.C. AL

ACCESSIBLE TUNE, THROUGHCOMPOSED FORM.

JUST IN TIME

COUNT BASIE & HIS ORCHESTRA & ROSEMARY CLOONEY, AT LONG LAST, CONCORD RECORDS, INC., 1998.

EXCELLENT EXAMPLE OF POLYRHYTHM.
JOSHUA
MILES DAVIS, SEVEN STEPS TO HEAVEN, 1963.
(FAST SWING)
- VICTOR FELDMAN
(BASS)
A
D-
(BS. CONT. SIMILE)
D-9 C-9 Bb-9 C-9 D-9
1.
2.
G-7 C7
B
Fmaj7 F-7 Bb7alt Ebmaj7 Eb-7 Ab7alt
Dbmaj7 N.C. Cmaj9#11 Bb-7 F/E A13b9 TO
(PNO.)

C
D-
(BASS, AS IN INTRO)
D-9
C-9
Bb-9
C-9
D-9
D
SOLOS
D-7
8
C-7
Bb-7
C-7
D-7
1.
2.
G-7
C7
Fmaj7
F-7
Bb7#5
Ebmaj7
Eb-7
Ab7alt
Dbmaj7
G7#5
C-7
Bb-7
E7alt
A7alt
PLAY 3X
D-7
8
C-7
Bb-7
C-7
D-7
AFTER SOLOS, D.S. AL
(TAKE REPEAT)
D-11
G-7
Db/G
Dbadd9/G
D-6/9
(BASS, AS IN INTRO)
(BS. ONLY)

GREAT RHYTHM SECTION ARRANGING.

JOSIE

(MED.)

STEELY DAN, AJA, UMG RECORDS, INC., 1977.

- WALTER BECKER/DONALD FAGEN

CHORUS
F#7#9
B7#5
E-7
C/F
F#7#9
B7#5
E-7
A7
A-7
D7
Gmaj7
Cmaj7
INTERLUDE
F#7#9
B7#5
TO
1.
E-7
BRIDGE
2.
8VA
N.C.
(GUITARS)
(8VA)
F#7#9
B7#9
D.S. AL
INTERLUDE
N.C.
(GUITARS)
C/F
F#7#9
D/G
Abmaj13
OUTRO/GUITAR SOLO
E-7
REPEAT AND FADE
(HORNS)

KILLER JOE

QUINCY JONES, ONE DAY FOREVER, ARKADIA ENTERTAINMENT CORP. 1996.

(MED.)

- BENNY GOLSON

C7(13) Bb7(13) C7(13) Bb7(13)

HEAD

C7 Bb7 C7 Bb7

C7 Bb7 C7 Bb7

E-7b5 A7b9 Eb-7 Ab7sus4 Ab7b9

A7(13) Ab7sus4 Ab7 E-7 E-7/A A7b9

C7 Bb7 C7 Bb7

C7 Bb7 C7 Bb7

REPEAT AND FADE

C7 Bb7 C7 Bb7

TYPICAL, ACCESSIBLE BEBOP TUNE GOOD FOR BASIC IMPROVISATION.

LADY BIRD

CHET BAKER, CHET BAKER IN MILAN, FANTASY, INC., 1959.

(MED. SWING)

- TADD DAMERON

Cmaj7 | | F-7 | Bb7 |

Cmaj7 | | Bb-7 | Eb7 |

Abmaj7 | | A-7 | D7 |

D-7 | G7 | Cmaj7 Eb7 | TO ⊕ Abmaj7 Db7#11 :|

REPEAT HEAD IN/OUT
AFTER SOLOS, D.C. AL ⊕

⊕ Abmaj7 Db7#11 | Cmaj7 ||

INTERESTING POP TUNE WITH GOOD HARMONIC MOTION. SOUNDS LIKE IT IS DIATONIC, BUT THE CADENCES GO TO UNEXPECTED KEYS.

KILLING ME SOFTLY WITH HIS SONG

ROBERTA FLACK, KILLING ME SOFTLY, RECORDING CORPORATION, 1973.

(MED. SLOW)

- NORMAN GIMBEL/CHARLES FOX

INTRO

F-7 Bb-7 | Eb Ab

F-7 Bb/D | Eb Db

Ab Db | Gbmaj7#11 F

Ebsus4 Eb7 | Eb7sus4 Eb7

VERSE

Bb-7 Eb7 | Abmaj7 Dbmaj7

Bb-7 Eb | F-7

Bb-7 Eb7 | Ab C7

CHORUS
F-7
Bb-7
Eb
Ab
F-7
Bb/D
Eb
Db
Ab
Db
Gbmaj7
TO
F
PLAY 3X
INTERLUDE
F-7
Bb-7
Eb
Ab
F-7
Bb/D
Eb
Db
Ab
Db
Gbmaj7
F
D.S. AL
F
OUTRO
F-7
Bb-7
Eb
Ab
F-7
Bb/D
Eb
Db
Ab
Db
Gbmaj7
F

GREAT HORN LINES.

KNOCK ON WOOD

E N.C.
TO
E
G
A
B
D
1.
B
2.
B A G N.C.
INTERLUDE
F#7
G#7
(HORNS)
A7
D.S. AL
C N.C.
B N.C.
E
G
A
B
D
B A G N.C.
OUTRO
E
A
E
A
REPEAT AND FADE

LAIRD BAIRD

CHARLIE PARKER, CHARLIE PARKER (VERVE), THE VERVE MUSIC GROUP, 1947.

- CHARLIE PARKER

(MED. FAST SWING)

Bb | A-7b5 D7 | G-7 Gb7 | F-7 Bb7 | Eb7 | Eb-7 Ab7 | TO ⊕ D-7 | Db-7 | C-7 | F7 | Bb G7 |

OPEN: C-7 F7 (REPEAT FOR SOLOS) | FINAL: C-7 F7 | LAST X, D.S. AL ⊕

⊕ D-7 | Db-7 Gb7 | C-7 F7 F#7 | Bb | Bb6

HYBRIDS, FOUR TONIC SYSTEM, HARMONIC SEQUENCE.
LAKES
PAT METHENY, WATERCOLORS, ECM RECORDS, 1977.
- PAT METHENY
UP (EVEN 8th's)
INTRO
D
A/D
G/D
A/D
HEAD
D
A/C#
B-
D/A
E/G#
G/A
Dmaj7
F#7
B-7
E-
G/A
A/G
Dmaj7/F#
E-9
G/A
Bb/A
A
Bbo7
B-
D/C
A/C#
A-7/D
Gmaj7
F#/G#
C#-7
C9
B-
D9
Gmaj7
F#-7
Fmaj7
E-9
F#-7
F#/G
E7#9/G#
Eb/A
D/A#
C/B
Bb/C
A7/C#
D9
D/Eb
E-9
F#-7
Gmaj7
A7sus4
D
(LAST X)
FINE
SOLOS
D
A/D
G/D
A/D
Dmaj7
C7sus4
Fmaj7
Ab7sus4
Dbmaj7
B7sus4
Emaj7
D7sus4
Gmaj7
F7sus4
Bbmaj7
Db7sus4
Gbmaj7
G7sus4
Cmaj7
A7sus4
AFTER SOLOS, D.S. AL FINE

BEBOP BALLAD, MINOR KEY AND PARALLEL MAJOR, ABAB.

EXAMPLE FROM AMERICAN THEATER.
LIDA ROSE
(FREELY)
ROBERT PRESTON & BARBARA COOK, THE MUSIC MAN, RIVER RECORDS, 2008.
- MEREDITH WILLSON
A
B

EXAMPLE FROM THE LATE BAROQUE ERA.

C/E C7/E F D-/F C/G G C
G7 C
G7 C C7/E F C C/Bb
F C7 F
C/G Gsus4 G
C Csus2 4 C/Bb F/A D7/A C/G G C
B
C G7 C G7 C G7 C G7 C
C7 F/C C7 F/C
G7/D C G7 C G7 C G7

C G7 C C7 F C F C
C7
C
F Bb/F
F F/C C7/E F D- Bb C Bb/F F
F/C C7/E F D- Bb C F C7/E
F/Eb Bb/D G7
D
C
G/D G7
G7/D C7/E
C7 F G-/F F

Bb/F C7/F F G- A G-/Bb F/A G-/Bb F/C C
F C7 F
C7 F F7/A Bb
F F7 Bb F7 Bb
G-/F
F/C C#o7 D- F/A Bb G7/B F/C
Csus4 C
E
F Fsus2/4 F/Eb
(STRINGS)
Bb/D Bo/D F/C C7 F

A GOOD EXAMPLE OF THE VERSE/REFRAIN ABBA FORM.

LET HIM FLY

(MED.)

PATTY GRIFFIN, LIVING WITH GHOSTS, UMG RECORDINGS, INC., 1996.

- PATTY GRIFFIN

B-
B-7
G
A
D
B-
F#-7
E-7
A
D/A
A
VERSE
D
Dsus2/F#
G
B-
G
E-7
A
OUTRO-CHORUS
D
G
D
G
D
G
D
G
D
G
D
G
D

BASED ON CHORD PROGRESSIONS FROM THE JAZZ STANDARDS REPERTOIRE.

LIKE SOMEONE IN LOVE

ELLA FITZGERALD, LIKE SOMEONE IN LOVE, THE VERVE MUSIC GROUP, 1957.

(MED.)

- JOHNNY BURKE/JIMMY VAN HEUSEN

SWING-ERA TUNE, SOME SECONDARY DOMINANTS, ABAC FORM.

LIMEHOUSE BLUES

DJANGO REINHARDT, CRAZY RHYTHM, MBOPGLOBAL-DELTA, 1996.

(FAST SWING)

- DOUGLAS FURBER/PHILLIP BRAHAM

Db9

Bb7

Abmaj7 C7 F-

Bb7 Eb7 D9

Db9

Bb7

Abmaj7 F7 Bb-7

Bb-7b5 Eb7 Ab6 (D9)

FINE

BEBOP HEAD, AABA, WITH II V'S, GOOD TRAINING TUNE FOR INTERMEDIATE PLAYERS.

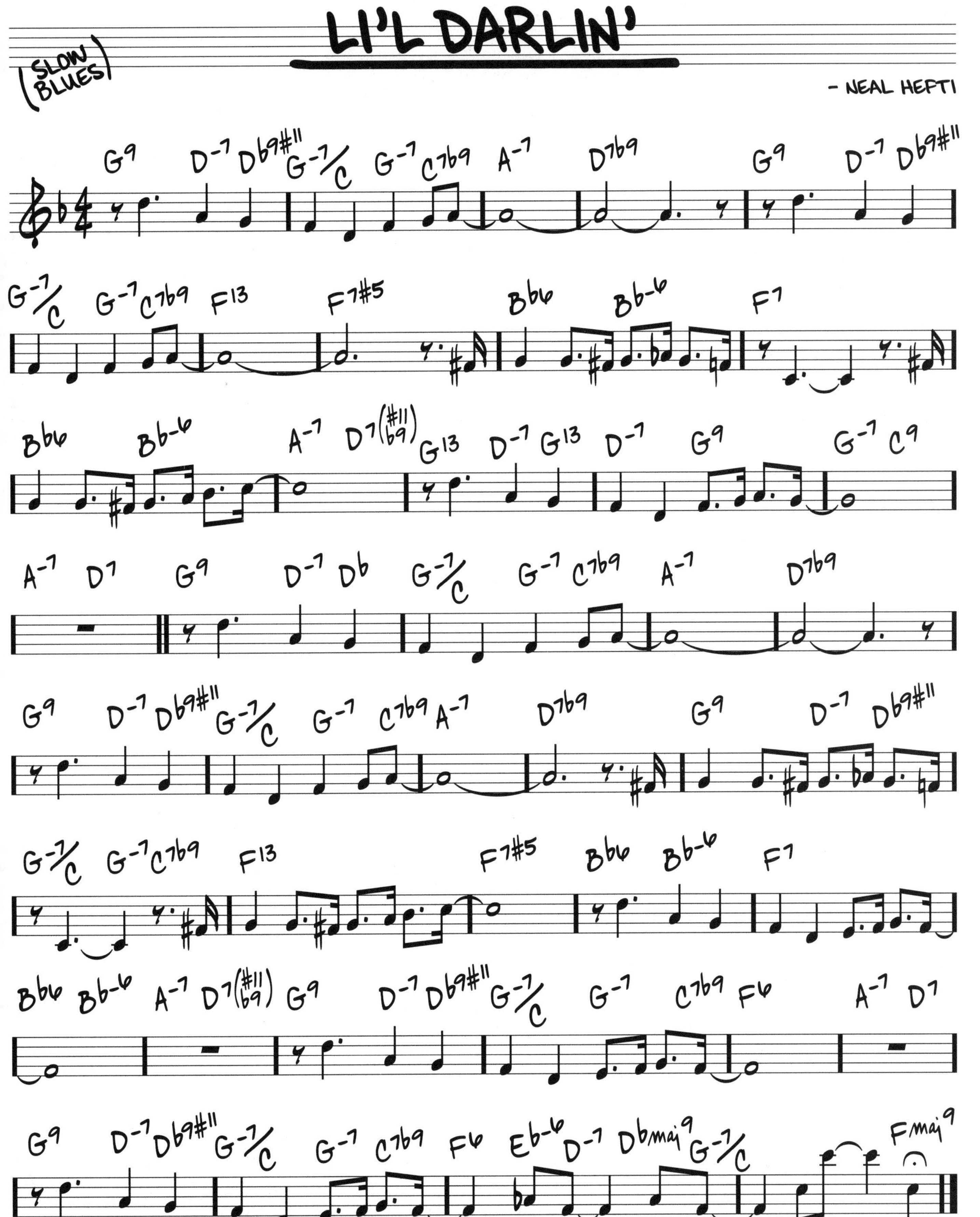
LI'L DARLIN'
(SLOW BLUES)
- NEAL HEFTI
G9 D-7 Db9#11 G-7/C G-7 C7b9 A-7 D7b9 G9 D-7 Db9#11
G-7/C G-7 C7b9 F13 F7#5 Bb6 Bb-6 F7
Bb6 Bb-6 A-7 D7(#11 b9) G13 D-7 G13 D-7 G9 G-7 C9
A-7 D7 G9 D-7 Db G-7/C G-7 C7b9 A-7 D7b9
G9 D-7 Db9#11 G-7/C G-7 C7b9 A-7 D7b9 G9 D-7 Db9#11
G-7/C G-7 C7b9 F13 F7#5 Bb6 Bb-6 F7
Bb6 Bb-6 A-7 D7(#11 b9) G9 D-7 Db9#11 G-7/C G-7 C7b9 F6 A-7 D7
G9 D-7 Db9#11 G-7/C G-7 C7b9 F6 Eb-6 D-7 Dbmaj9 G-7/C Fmaj9

DORIAN HARMONY WITH LYDIAN AND IONIAN MODAL INTERCHANGE.
LITTLE SUNFLOWER
(MED. LATIN)
FREDDIE HUBBARD, BACKLASH, ATLANTIC RECORDING CORP., 1966.
- FREDDIE HUBBARD
INTRO
D-
(BASS)
HEAD
D-7
BS. CONT. SIM.
1.
2.
Eb maj7
D maj7
1.
2.
D-7
TAKE REPEATS ON SOLOS
AFTER SOLOS, LAST HEAD, VAMP INTRO TO FADE

USES I VI II V PROGRESSION IN TWO KEYS.

LONG AGO (AND FAR AWAY)

GENE AMMONS AND SONNY STITT., BOSS TENORS IN ORBIT, UMVD, 1962.

(BALLAD)

- IRA GERSHWIN/JEROME KERN

C6 A-7 D-7 G7 CMAJ7 D-7 G7

C6 D-7 G7 E-7 A7 D-7 G7

1. Eb6 C-7 F-7 Bb7 EbMAJ7 D7

GMAJ7 E-7 A7 D-7 G7

2. G-7 C7 FMAJ7 Bb9

C6/E Eb°7 D-7 G7 C6 (D-7 G7)

MODAL INTERCHANGE.
LOOK TO THE SKY
WAVE, UMG RECORDINGS, INC., 1967.
- ANTONIO CARLOS JOBIM
(BOSSA)
A
Ebmaj7
Eb-7
Ab7
Ebmaj7
G-7
C7b9
F-7
Ab-7
Db7
G-7
Gbo7
F-7
Bb7#5
B
Ebmaj7
Eb-7
Ab7
Ebmaj7
G-7
C7b9
F-7
Ab-7
Db7
Gbmaj7
Emaj7#11
TO
Ebmaj7
AFTER SOLOS, D.C. AL
Ebmaj7
G-7
C7b9
F-7
Emaj7#11
Ebmaj7
Ab-7
Db7b9
Gbmaj7
Emaj7#11
Ebmaj7

LOVE IN VAIN BLUES
(SLOW SHUFFLE)
- ROBERT JOHNSON
INTRO
G
G°7
D7
G G/F G/E G/Eb
(GUITAR)
G/D D7
VERSE
G
G7
C
G7 D7
G
A7
D7
TO
G G/F G/E G/Eb
1., 2.
G/D D7
3.
G/D G7
D.S. AL
G G7/F G/E G/Eb G/D D7 G

LOVE WALKED IN
(MED.)
- GEORGE GERSHWIN/IRA GERSHWIN
C A-7 D7 D-7 G7
C A-7 D7 G7
C7sus4 C7 F6#11 A7
D-7 F-7 G7 E-7 A7(b13 b9) D7 D-7 G7
C A-7 D7 D-7 G7
C A-7 D7 G7
C7sus4 C7 F6 F#-7b5 B7(b13 b9)
E-7 A7b9 D-7 G7b9 C6

AABA FORM.

LOVER MAN
(OH, WHERE CAN YOU BE?)

(BALLAD)

BILLIE HOLIDAY, THE COMPLETE DECCA RECORDINGS, UMG RECORDINGS, INC., 1944.

- JIMMY DAVIS/ROGER RAMIREZ/JIMMY SHERMAN

INTERESTING HARMONIES, GOOD FOR PRACTICING REHARMONIZATION, OFTEN PLAYED VERY FAST.
AABA FORM, SOMETIMES PLAYED AS 64-BAR TUNE, RATHER THAN 32.
EXAMPLE OF AN INTERPRETATION CHANGING THE METER, FROM THE ORIGINAL 3/4 TO 4/4.

LOVER

WYNTON MARSALIS, STANDARD TIME, VOL. 2: INTIMACY CALLING, SONY MUSIC ENTERTAINMENT, INC., 1987.

(UP)

- LORENZ HART/RICHARD ROGERS

G maj7
Ab o7
A-7
D7
Bb maj7
B o7
C-7
F7
G-7
C7
F-7
Bb7
Eb maj7
A-7
D7
Ab-7
Db7
G-7
C7
Gb-7
Cb7
F-7
TO ⊕
Bb7
Eb6
(SOLO BREAK)
(C-7
F-7
Bb7)
AFTER SOLOS, D.C. AL ⊕
(TAKE REPEAT)
⊕
Bb7
Eb6
N.C.

BEBOP, AABA, MINOR TO RELATIVE MAJOR.
DIATONIC AND SECONDARY DOMINANTS HARMONY.

LULLABY OF BIRDLAND

MINOR KEY, BRIDGE GOES INTO PARALLEL MAJOR.

LULLABY OF THE LEAVES

(MED.)

CHET BAKER, PRINCE OF COOL: THE PACIFIC JAZZ YEARS (1952-57), BLUE NOTE RECORDS, 1952.

- JOE YOUNG/BERNICE PETKERE

BALLAD, SOPHISTICATED HARMONICALLY AND MELODICALLY.
LUSH LIFE
JOHN COLTRANE AND JOHNNY HARTMAN, JOHAN COLTRANE AND JOHNNY HARTMAN, UMG RECORDINGS, INC., 1963.
(BALLAD)
- BILLY STRAYHORN
Db6 Cb7 Dbmaj7 Cb7
Dbmaj7 C7 Dbmaj7 Eb-7 F-7 Gb-7
Ab-7 D7 F-7 D7
1. D-b9 D7b5
2. D-b9 G-7b5 C7
F- F-6 F-7 F-
G-7 Gb7b5 F- F-6 F-7
F- Ab7 B7b5

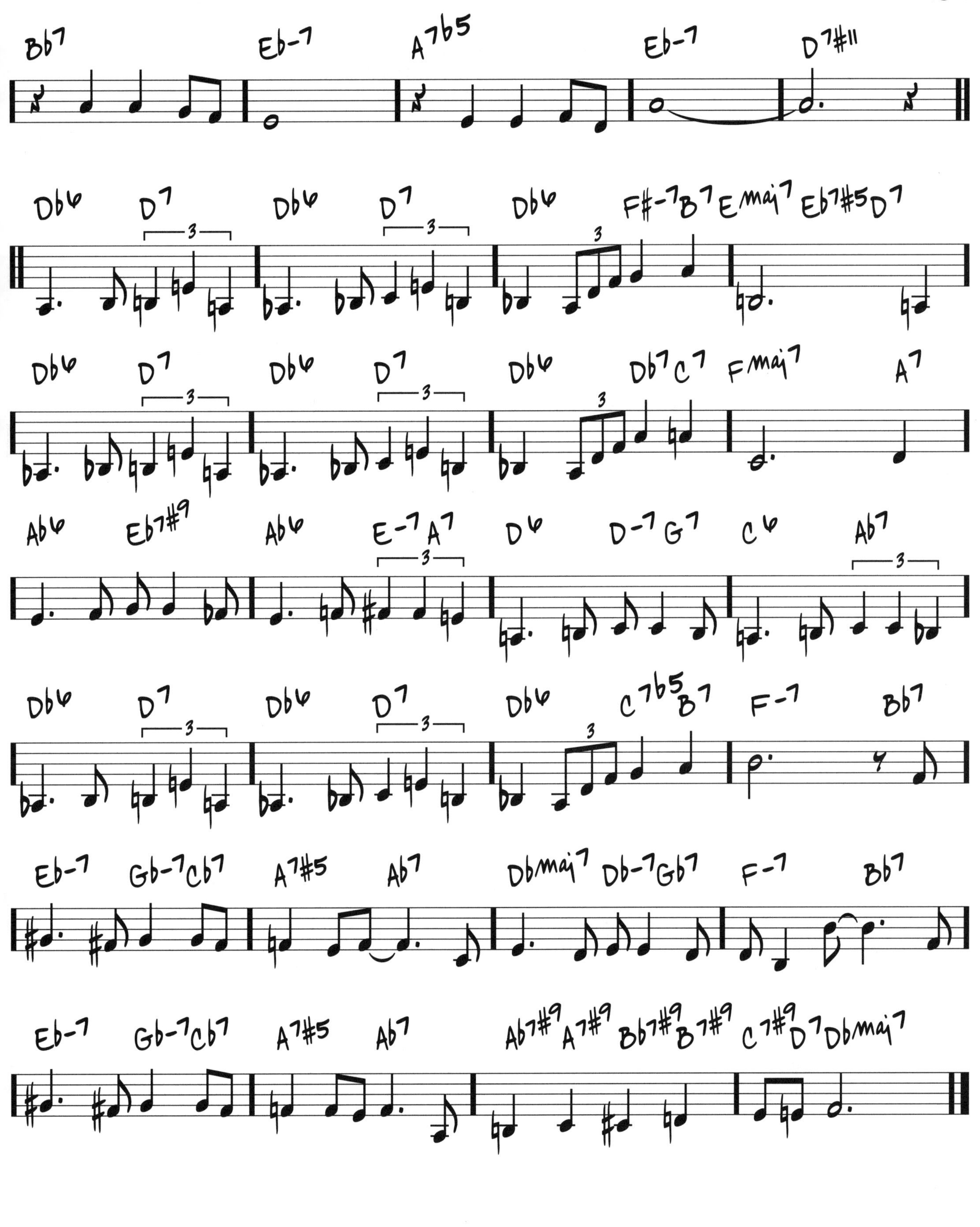
Bb7 Eb-7 A7b5 Eb-7 D7#11
Db6 D7 Db6 D7 Db6 F#-7 B7 Emaj7 Eb7#5 D7
Db6 D7 Db6 D7 Db6 Db7 C7 Fmaj7 A7
Ab6 Eb7#9 Ab6 E-7 A7 D6 D-7 G7 C6 Ab7
Db6 D7 Db6 D7 Db6 C7b5 B7 F-7 Bb7
Eb-7 Gb-7 Cb7 A7#5 Ab7 Dbmaj7 Db-7 Gb7 F-7 Bb7
Eb-7 Gb-7 Cb7 A7#5 Ab7 Ab7#9 A7#9 Bb7#9 B7#9 C7#9 D7 Dbmaj7

SOPHISTICATED HARMONICALLY.
MAHJONG
JUJU, BLUE NOTE RECORDS, 1999.
(MED. AFRO-LATIN/SWING)
- WAYNE SHORTER
INTRO
(AFRO/LATIN)
F-11
Eb6/9
F-11
Eb6/9
(OPT: START W/OPEN DRUMS, ADD PNO./BS., REPEAT 2X)
HEAD
F-11
Eb6/9
F-11
Eb6/9
F-11
Eb6/9
F-11
Eb6/9
Dbmaj9
Eb6/9
Dbmaj9
Eb6/9
Dbmaj9
Eb6/9
Dbmaj9
Eb6/9
(SWING)
D7#9
Eb-7
Ab7
Dbmaj7
Db-7
Gb7
(AFRO/LATIN)
F-11
Eb6/9
F-11
Eb6/9
F-11
Eb6/9
F-11
Eb6/9
AFTER SOLOS/LAST HEAD,
VAMP INTRO TILL END

IMPROVISATION ON OSTINATO AND SUS4 CHORDS.
MAIDEN VOYAGE
MED. (EVEN 8TH'S)
HERBIE HANCOCK, MAIDEN VOYAGE, BLUE NOTE RECORDS, 1999.
- HERBIE HANCOCK
INTRO
D9sus4
F9sus4
(MELODY)
HEAD
D9sus4
(CONT. RHYTHM SIM.)
F9sus4
1.
2.
Eb9sus4
Db-6/9
D9sus4
F9sus4
AFTER SOLOS, LAST HEAD, VAMP INTRO TILL END

AABA VERSE/REFRAIN WITH A PRIMARY BRIDGE SONG;
ORDER OF PHRASES: AAAB.

MAKE YOU FEEL MY LOVE

(SLOW)

BOB DYLAN, TIME OUT OF MIND, SONY MUSIC ENTERTAINMENT INC., 1997.

Eb9
Gb/Ab
Db
BRIDGE
Gb
Db/Ab
A+
Gb/Bb
C°7
Db
Gb
Db
Eb9
Gb/Ab
Ab
VERSE
Db
Ab/C
Ab-/Cb
Gb
Gb-
Db
Eb9
Gb/Ab
Db

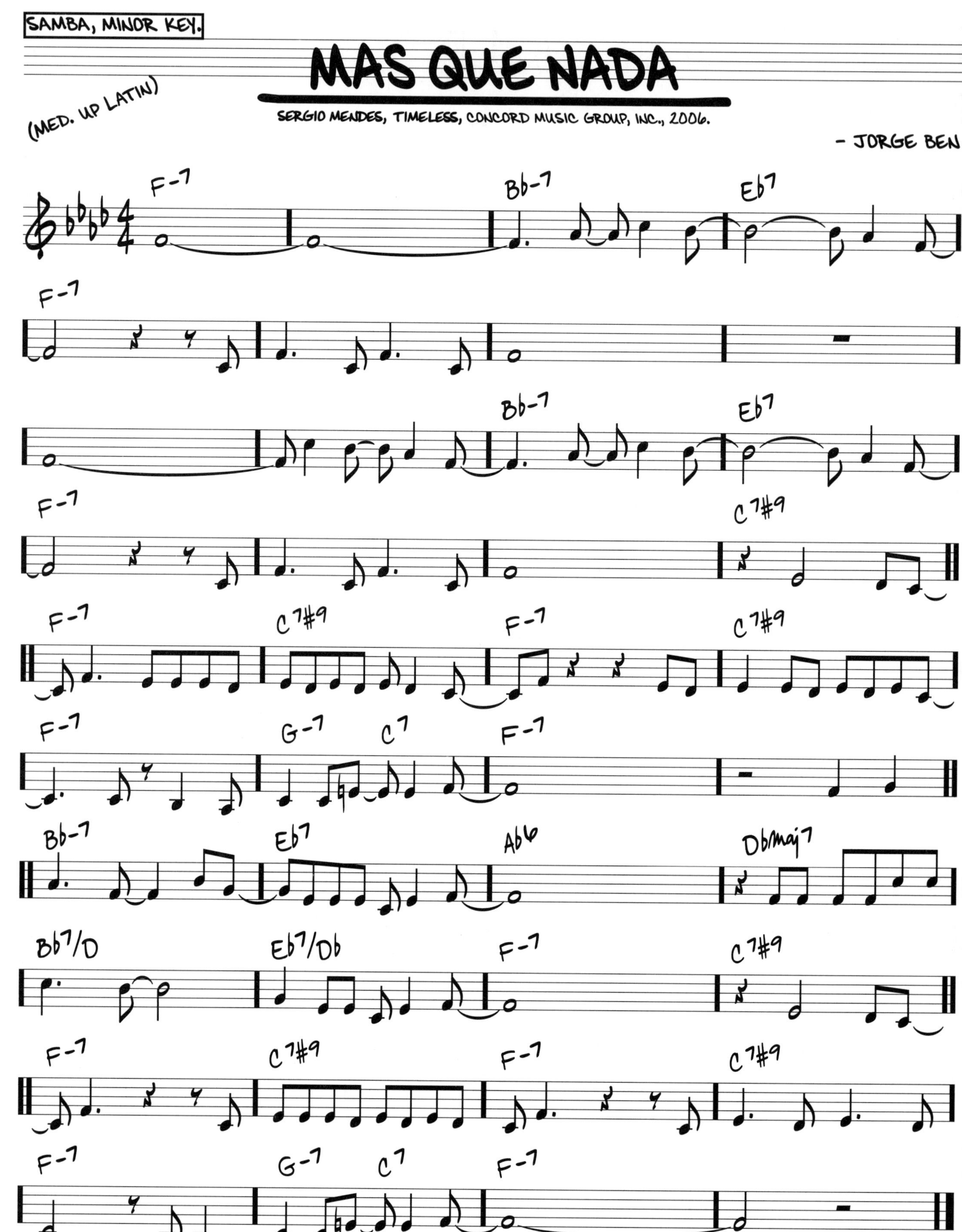
SAMBA, MINOR KEY.
MAS QUE NADA
(MED. UP LATIN)
SERGIO MENDES, TIMELESS, CONCORD MUSIC GROUP, INC., 2006.
- JORGE BEN
F-7
Bb-7
Eb7
F-7
Bb-7
Eb7
F-7
C7#9
F-7
C7#9
F-7
C7#9
F-7
G-7
C7
F-7
Bb-7
Eb7
Ab6
Dbmaj7
Bb7/D
Eb7/Db
F-7
C7#9
F-7
C7#9
F-7
C7#9
F-7
G-7
C7
F-7

MODAL INTERCHANGE.
MIMOSA
(MED. JAZZ)
EARL KLUGH & GEORGE BENSON, COLLABORATION 2000, SONY BMG MUSIC ENTERTAINMENT, 2004.
- GEORGE BENSON
A
TO
B
AFTER SOLOS, D.C. AL
SOLOS ON B
C SOLO
REPEAT AND FADE

MINOR BLUES, ACCESSIBLE.

MR. P.C.

(BRIGHT JAZZ)

GIANT STEPS, ATLANTIC RECORDING CORPORATION, 1959.

- JOHN COLTRANE

C-

F-

C-

Ab7

G7(b13 b9)

C-

STUDY OF II V MOTION MOVING THROUGH VARIOUS KEY AREAS.
MISTY
(BALLAD)
SARAH VAUGHAN, MISTY, UMG RECORDINGS INC., 1958.
- ERROLL GARNER
CMaj7
G-7
C7
FMaj7
F-7
Bb7
CMaj7
A-7
D-7
G7
E-7
A7
D-7
G7
C6
Bb9
CMaj7
G-7
C7b9
FMaj7
F#-7
B7
D7
E-7
A7b9
D-7
G7
CMaj7
G-7
C7
FMaj7
F-7
Bb7
CMaj7
A-7
D-7
G7
C6
(A-7
D-7
G7)

GOOD FOR PRACTICING II V'S.

MOMENT'S NOTICE

(UP)

2.
G-7
C7#9
F-7
Bb7
Eb/Bb
F-/Bb
G-/Bb
F-/Bb
Eb/Bb
F-/Bb
G-/Bb
F-/Bb
TO
Eb (SOLO BREAK)
SOLOS ON B, TAKE REPEAT
CHORDS PLAYED ON BEAT
AFTER SOLOS, D.S. AL (TAKE REPEAT)
Eb7#9

GREAT EXAMPLE OF A LATIN JAZZ TUNE, WITH A NON-STANDARD FORM AND A GREAT ARRAY OF CHORD PROGRESSIONS.

MOON AND SAND

(MED. BOSSA)

KENNY BURRELL, GUITAR FORMS, POLYGRAM RECORDS, 1995 (1965).

- ALEC WILDER/MORTY PALITZ/WILLIAM ENGVICK

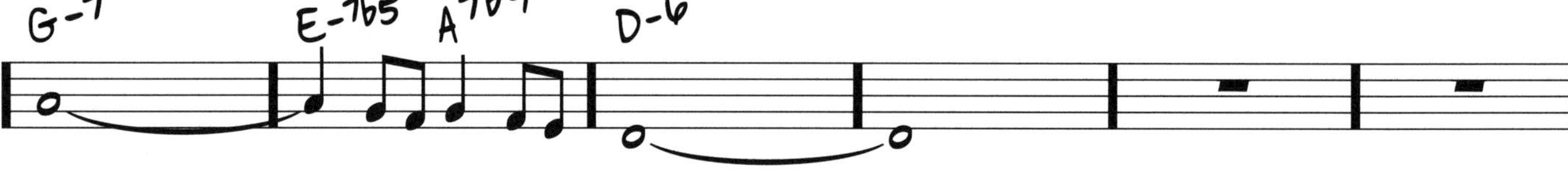

CLASSIC BALLAD.
MOONLIGHT IN VERMONT
(BALLAD)
FRANK SINATRA, COME FLY WITH ME, CAPITOL RECORDS, INC., 1957.
- JOHN BLACKBURN/KARL SUESSDORF
Eb6 C-7 F-7 Bb7 Eb6 C-7
Db7 F-7 Bb7sus4 1. Eb6 Bb7sus4 2. Eb6
A-7 D7 Gmaj7 E7b9 A-7 D7 Gmaj7
Bb-7 Eb7 Abmaj7 F7b9 Bb-7 Eb7 Abmaj7 Bb7b9
Eb6 C-7 F-7 Bb7 Eb6 C-7 Db7
TO ⊕
F-7 Bb7sus4 Eb6 (Bb7sus4)
AFTER SOLOS, D.S. AL ⊕
(TAKE REPEAT)
Eb6 C7#9 F7 E7 Ebmaj7
RIT.

MOTEN SWING
(MED. SWING)
- BUSTER MOTEN/BENNIE MOTEN
Ab6 Bb-7
Eb7 Bb7 Bb-7/Eb
1. Ab6 F7b9 Bb7 Eb7 2. Ab6
D-7 G7 C6 A-7 D-7 G7
C6 A-7 D-7 G7 C6 A-7
D-7 G7 C6 Bb-7 Eb7
Ab6 Bb-7
Eb7 Bb7 Bb-7/Eb
Ab6 (F7b9 Bb7b9 Eb7b9)

FAST-MOVING BEBOP HEAD.

MOVE

(UP)

GEORGE SHEARING, SEPTEMBER IN THE RAIN, VERVE, 2003 (2000).

- DENZIL DE COSTA BEST

EXAMPLE FROM MUSICAL THEATER.

THE MUSIC OF THE NIGHT

THE PHANTOM OF THE OPERA (ORIGINAL CAST RECORDING), THE REALLY USEFUL GROUP, 1987.

Gb
Db
Gb
Db
Gb
Cb
Db/Ab
Gb/Ab
Ab7
RIT.
A TEMPO
Db
B
E
A
Eb
Ab
Ab7
RIT.
Db
SLOWLY
F-
C
F
D.C. AL
Gb
Cb
Gb
Db/Ab
Gb/Ab
Ab7
Db
Ab/Db
Db
Ab/Db
Db
Gb
Ab7
Gb
Db
Gb
Db
Gb
Cb
Gb
Db/Ab
POCO RIT.
Gb/Ab
Ab7
Gb
Eb
D-
C
Db

GREAT HORN LINES.

MUSTANG SALLY

(MED. FUNK)

WILSON PICKETT, THE WICKED PICKETT, ATLANTIC RECORDING CORP., 1997.

- BONNY RICE

F7
C7
G7
F7
N.C.
C7
(HORNS)
VERSE
C7
D.S.
(FADE ON CHORUS)

EXAMPLE OF '90S POP BALLAD WITH CHARACTERISTIC MINOR KEY HARMONIC DEVICES.

MY ALL

MARIAH CAREY, BUTTERFLY, SONY MUSIC ENTERTAINMENT, 1997.

- MARIAH CAREY/WALTER AFANASIEFF

(SLOW BALLAD)

INTRO

N.C. (GUITAR) | C- | D7 |

G- | | C- |

D7 | Gsus4 G | |

VERSE

N.C. | C-7 | D |

G- | | C-7 |

D | G- | G-/F |

Eb | D7sus4 D7 | G- |

CHORUS
N.C.
C-7
D7sus4
D7
G-
G-/F
Ebmaj7
C-7
F7
Bbmaj7
Ebmaj7
A-7b5
Ab7#11
G-
G-/F
E-7b5
C-7
TO
D
1.
G-
2.
G-
D.S. AL
D
G-
G-/F
Ebmaj7
C-7
D
N.C.
G-
C-7
D
RIT.
G-

EXAMPLE FROM AMERICAN MUSICAL THEATER.

MY FAVORITE THINGS

(MED. FAST)

THE SOUND OF MUSIC (ORIGINAL SOUNDTRACK), 1964.

- OSCAR HAMMERSTEIN II / RICHARD RODGERS

E-7 F#-7 E-7 F#-7 C maj7

A-7 D7

G maj7 C maj7 G maj7 C maj7 F#-7b5 B7

E maj7 F#-7 E maj7 F#-7 A maj7

A7 G maj7 C6

D7 G6 C maj7 G6 C maj7

G maj7 C maj7 F#-7b5 B7 (END) E-7

D.C. FOR SOLOS

MY FUNNY VALENTINE

(BALLAD)

SARAH VAUGHAN, LIVE IN JAPAN, VOLUME 1, MAINSTREAM RECORDS, 1991.

- LORENZ HART/RICHARD RODGERS

CLASSIC AABA FORM, CATCHY MELODY THAT'S A GREAT STUDY IN SYNCOPATION.

MY LITTLE SUEDE SHOES

CHARLIE PARKER, BIRD: THE COMPLETE CHARLIE PARKER ON VERVE, THE VERVE MUSIC GROUP, 1988.

- CHARLIE PARKER

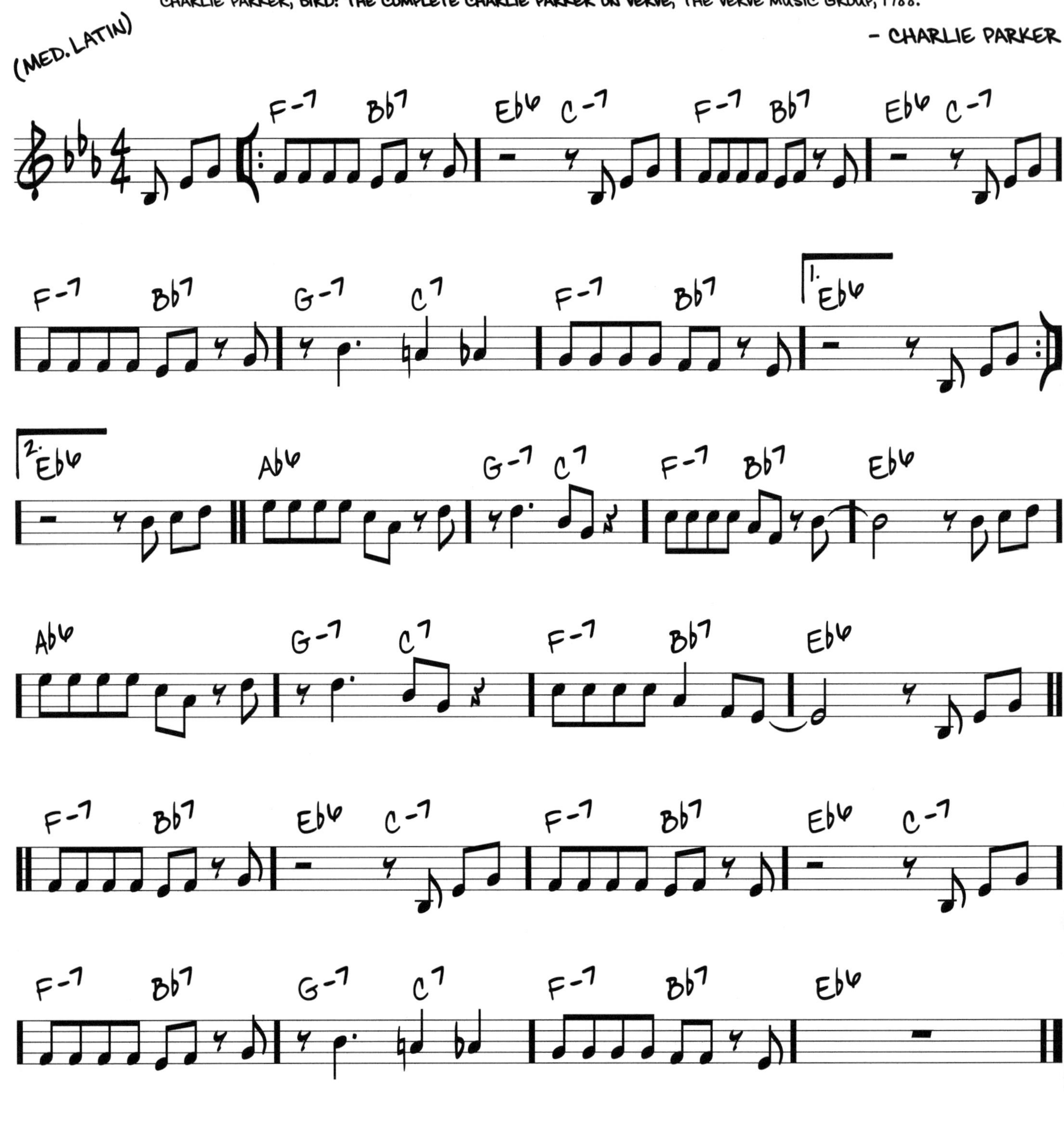

MY MAN (MON HOMME)

FROM ZIEGFELD FOLLIES

(SLOW SWING)

- MAURICE YVAIN/ALBERT WILLEMETZ/
JACQUES CHARLES/CHANNING POLLOCK

INTRO

F- Db/F F-6 Db/F G-7b5

C7b9 1. F-

2. F- Eb

Db7 C7#5 Eb7 HEAD Ab6

Eb7 Bb-7 Eb7

Abmaj7 Eb7 Ab6 Eb-7 Ab7

Dbmaj7 Do7 Abmaj7/Eb F-7 Bb7 Eb7

Ab6 (Bb-7 Eb7)

FINE

D.S. FOR SOLOS
AFTER SOLOS, D.S. AL FINE

SECONDARY DOMINANTS, LINE CLICHÉS.
MY ROMANCE
(MODERATE OR BALLAD)
THE RAY BROWN TRIO, THREE DIMENSIONAL, CONCORD JAZZ, INC., 1991.
- LORENZ HART/RICHARD RODGERS
C maj7 F maj7 E-7 Eb°7 D-7 G7 C maj7 E7(b13 b9)
A-7 E7(b13 b9) A-7 A7 D-7 G7 1. C maj7 C7
F maj7 Bb7 C maj7 C7 F maj7 Bb7 C maj7
F#-7b5 B7b9 E-7 Bb7 A-7 D7 D-7 G7
2. C maj7 C7 F maj7 A7 D-7 D-7/C B-7b5 E7
A-7 Ab7 C maj7/G A-7 D-7 G7 C6
FINE
(D-7 G7)

BASED ON CHORD PROGRESSIONS FROM THE JAZZ STANDARDS REPERTOIRE.

(MED. BALLAD)

MY SHINING HOUR

JOHN COLTRANE, COLTRANE JAZZ, 1961.

- JOHNNY MERCER/HAROLD ARLEN

CMaj7 A-7 G7sus4 D-7 G7

CMaj7 A-7 A7#5 D-7 B-7b5 E7b9

A-7 B-7b5 E7

A-7 D7 D-7 G7

G-7 C7 FMaj7

F-7 Bb7 C6/E Ebo7 D-7 G7

CMaj7 D-7 G7sus4 CMaj7 D-7 E-7 A7

D-7 G7 C6 (D-7 G7)

HARMONICALLY ADVANCED, ABAC FORM.

NEVER LET ME GO

GEORGE SHEARING, SEPTEMBER IN THE RAIN, VERVE, 2003 (2000).

- JAY LIVINGSTON/RAY EVANS

MINOR KEY, AABA FORM, MOVES FROM BOSSA TO SWING. GOOD EXAMPLE OF EMBELLISHING A MOTIF; GREAT ARRANGEMENT WITH SOME NICE INTERLUDES.
NICA'S DREAM
(MED. LATIN/SWING)
HORACE SILVER, HORACE SCOPE, BLUE NOTE RECORDS, 2006 (1960).
- HORACE SILVER
A (LATIN)
Bb-(maj7)
Ab-(maj7)
Bb-(maj7)
Ab-7
Db7
Ab-7
Db7
Gbmaj7
Db9
C7#9
C-7b5/F
F7(b9 #5)
Bb-(maj7)
1.
(F7#5)
2. Bb
(FINE)
B (SWING)
Ab7sus4
Ab7
F-7
Bb7b9
Bb7#5
Eb9#11
Eb-7
Ab7
Dbmaj7
E-7
A7
Ab7sus4
Ab7
F-7
Bb7b9
Bb7#5
Eb9#11
Eb-7
Ab7
Dbmaj7
F7#5
N.C.
D.S. AL 2ND ENDING
SOLO A A B A
Music © 1956 by Ecaroh Music, Inc.
Copyright Renewed 1984
Words © 1994 by Ecaroh Music, Inc.

NEVER TOO MUCH

(MED. FUNK)

- LUTHER VANDROSS

E-7
G/A
A/B
G(maj7)
G/A
CHORUS
F#-/B
E-7
G
A6
F#-/B
E-7
G
A6
F#-/B
E-7
G
A6
F#-/B
E-7
G
TO
A6
N.C.
G/A
(GTR.)
D.S. AL
Gb/Ab
G/A
Ab/Bb
A/B
A6
F#-/B
D.S.S.
(FADE ON CHORUS)

EXTENDED FORM STANDARD USUALLY PLAYED WITH TRANSITIONS BETWEEN LATIN JAZZ AND SWING.

THE NIGHT HAS A THOUSAND EYES

JOHN COLTRANE, COLTRANE'S SOUND, ATLANTIC RECORDING CORPORATION, 1960.

- BUDDY BERNIER/JERRY BRAININ

A NIGHT IN TUNISIA

- JOHN "DIZZY" GILLESPIE/FRANK PAPARELLI

NIGHT TRAIN
(MED. SWING)
- OSCAR WASHINGTON/LEWIS C. SIMPKINS/JIMMY FORREST
A
Bb7
Eb7 E7 Eb7 Bb7
TO ⊕
Gb7 F7 Bb7
B
Bb7
Eb7 Bb7
C-7 F7 Bb7 F7 Bb6
C
N.C. F7 Bb6 N.C. F7
Bb6 N.C.

SOLO
Eb7
Bb7
D-7
G7
C-7
F7
Bb7
F7
SOLOS
Bb7
Eb7
Bb7
G7
C-7
F7
D-7
G7
C-7
F7
AFTER SOLOS, D.C. AL
C-7
F7
Ab7
G7
C-7
F7
Bb7
(PIANO-BASIE)
(BASS)

POP SONG, GOOD FOR PRACTICING ACCOMPANYING VOCALISTS; LISTENING TO LYRICS HELPS INVOLVE RHYTHM SECTION.

Dadd9 D Dadd9 D F♯-(add9) F♯- F♯-(add9) F♯-

BRIDGE

F♯-(add9) E/G♯ Dmaj7

Amaj7 G♯-7 C♯7 Dmaj7

D.S. AL ⊕
(TAKE 1st ENDING)

F♯- Dmaj7 Amaj7 G♯-7 C♯7

⊕ **INTERLUDE**

F♯- E/G♯ A Dmaj7 C♯7 PLAY 4X F♯- E/G♯ A Dmaj7 C♯7 PLAY 6X

F♯- E/G♯ Dmaj7 C♯-7 B-7 Amaj7 G♯7sus4 C♯7sus4

OUTRO

F♯-(add9) F♯- F♯-(add9) F♯- Eadd9 E Eadd9 E

(PIANO)

REPEAT AND FADE

Dadd9 D Dadd9 D F♯-(add9) F♯- F♯-(add9) F♯-

R&B BALLAD FEATURING CHARACTERISTIC HARMONIC AND RHYTHMIC DEVICES.

NOBODY'S SUPPOSED TO BE HERE

DEBORAH COX, ONE WISH, ARISTA RECORDS, 1998.

- ANTHONY CRAWFORD/MONTELL JORDAN

PRE-CHORUS
F7b9
Eb-9
Ab7
Dbmaj7
C-7
Bb-7
C-7
Dbmaj7
Bb-7
1. Db/Eb
D7(#11 #9)
2. Db/Eb
D/E
CHORUS
Dmaj7
F#-7
B-7
N.C.
C#-7
B-7
C7
C#-7
F#-7
N.C.
F-9
E-9
Eb7(#11 #9)
OUTRO-CHORUS
Dmaj7
F#-7
B-7
C-7
C#-7
F#-7
N.C.
F#-7
E-9
A7
Dmaj7
F#-7
B-7
C-7
REPEAT AND FADE
C#-7
F#-7
E-9
A7

EXCELLENT DRUM TONE DEVELOPMENT AND BALANCE WITHIN THE CONTEXT OF BRUSH PERFORMANCE.

(MED.)

(THERE IS) NO GREATER LOVE

AHMAD JAMAL TRIO, COMPLETE LIVE AT THE PERSHING LOUNGE 1958, GAMBIT SPAIN, 2007 (1958).

- MARTY SYMES/ISHAM JONES

EXAMPLE OF A "RHYTHM CHANGES" CONTRAFACT (BORROWED CHORD PROGRESSION). GREAT RHYTHMIC EMPHASIS POINTS.

SIMPLE FORM AND CHORDS, BUT A HAPPY TUNE.

ON THE SUNNY SIDE OF THE STREET

DIZZY GILLESPIE, SONNY ROLLINS, AND SONNY STITT, SONNY SIDE UP, THE VERVE MUSIC GROUP, 1957.

(SWING)

– DOROTHY FIELDS/JIMMY McHUGH

CLASSIC BOSSA NOVA

ONCE I LOVED

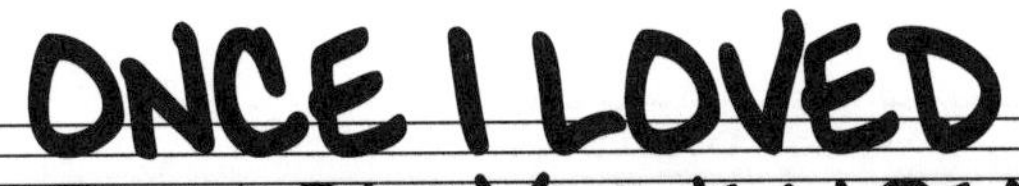

(AMOR EM PAZ) (LOVE IN PEACE)

(MED. BOSSA)

ANTONIO CARLOS JOBIM & ASTRUD GILBERTO, THE ASTRUD GILBERTO ALBUM, THE VERVE MUSIC GROUP, 1965.

- ANTONIO CARLOS JOBIM/VINICIUS DE MORAES/RAY GILBERT

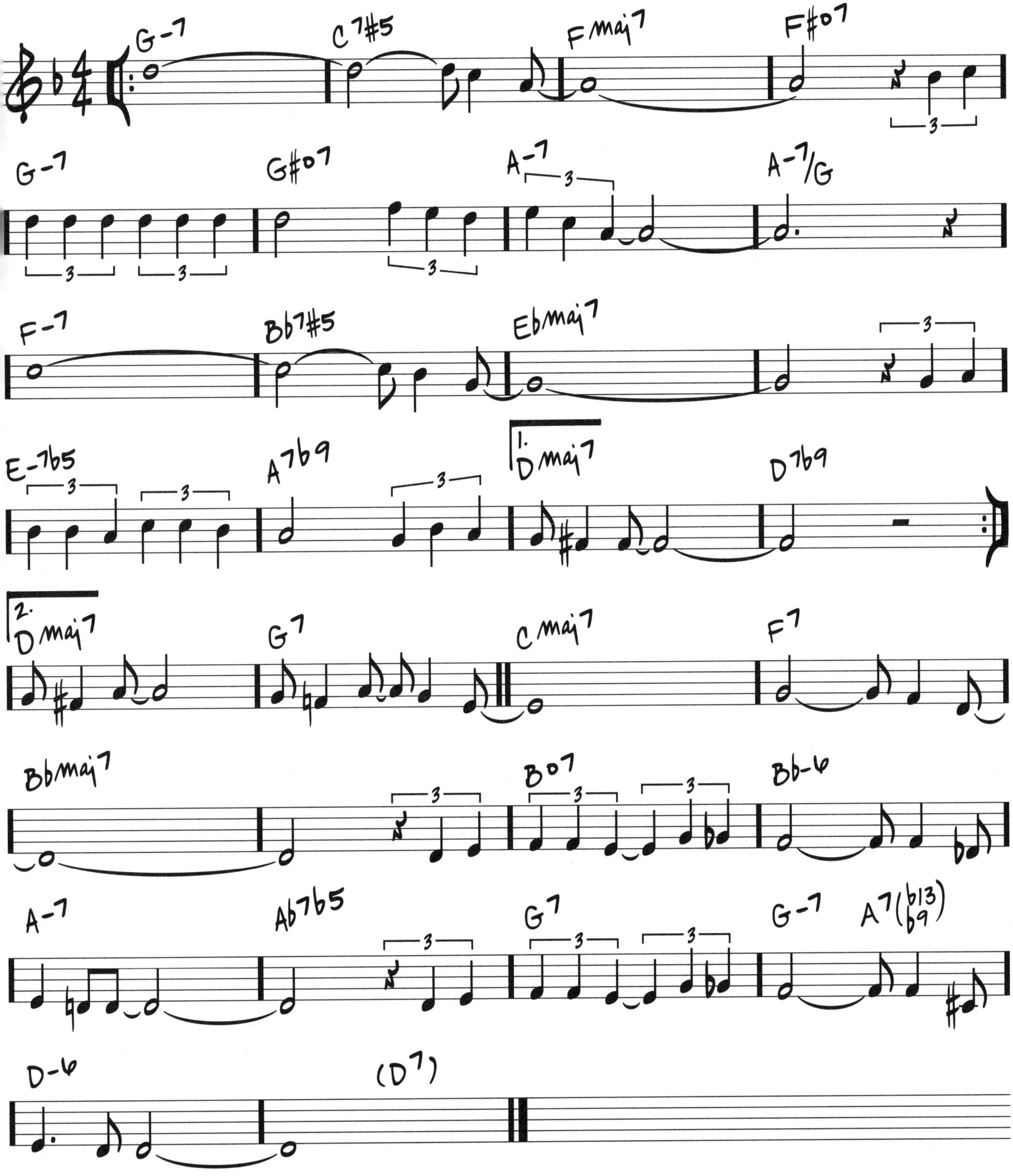
G-7
C7#5
Fmaj7
F#o7
G-7
G#o7
A-7
A-7/G
F-7
Bb7#5
Ebmaj7
E-7b5
A7b9
1. Dmaj7
D7b9
2. Dmaj7
G7
Cmaj7
F7
Bbmaj7
Bo7
Bb-6
A-7
Ab7b5
G7
G-7
A7(b13 b9)
D-6
(D7)

SOPHISTICATED TUNE, ADVANCED, FINGER BUSTER!

TONIC MODAL INTERCHANGE.

ONE NOTE SAMBA
(SAMBA DE UMA NOTA SO)

(MED. UP LATIN)

ANTONIO CARLOS JOBIM, THE COMPOSER OF "DESAFINADO," PLAYS, THE VERVE MUSIC GROUP, 1963.

– NEWTON MENDONÇA/ANTONIO CARLOS JOBIM

ORNITHOLOGY
(MED. UP)
- CHARLIE PARKER/BENNIE HARRIS
Gmaj7
G-7 C7 G-7 C7
Fmaj7
F-7
Bb7
Eb7
A-7b5 D7
1. G-7
D7
B-7
E7
A-7
D7
2. G
D7
B-7 Bb-7 A-7 Ab-7
G
(A-7 D7)
FINE

MAKES GOOD USE OF II V I PROGRESSION.

OUT OF NOWHERE

(MED.)

CHARLIE PARKER, THE GENIUS OF CHARLIE PARKER, SAVOY JAZZ, 1945.

– EDWARD HEYMAN/JOHNNY GREEN

GREAT HORN LINES.

PAPA'S GOT A BRAND NEW BAG

JAMES BROWN: THE 50TH ANNIVERSAY COLLECTION, UNIVERSAL RECORDS, 2003.

- JAMES BROWN

VERSE
Eb9
Ab7
Eb9
Bb7
Ab7 N.C.
Eb9
Bb7
OUTRO
Eb9
REPEAT AND FADE

HYBRIDS, POLYCHORDS, OSTINATOS.
PASSAGE
(MED. FUNK)
CHICK COREA'S ELECKTRIC BAND, EYE OF THE BEHOLDER, UMG RECORDS, INC., 1988.
- CHICK COREA
A INTRO
(RHYTHM SECTION)
(INSTRUMENTAL SOLO UNTIL HEAD)
(INSTRUMENTAL BACKGROUND)
B HEAD/SOLOS
(PIANO)
TO
Ab-7 Eb-7
Cbmaj7 Ab-/Bb
Ab/Bb
G/A
Fmaj7/G Ebmaj7/F Dmaj7#5/F# Cmaj7#5/E Absus2

Eb-7 Ab-7 Eb-7 Ab-7 Eb-7

Ab-7 Eb-7 Ab-7 Eb-7 Ab-7 Eb-7

AFTER SOLOS, D.S. AL ⊕

Ab-7 Eb-7 Ab-7 Eb-7 Cbmaj7 Ab-/Bb

⊕

Cbmaj7 Ab/Bb G/A Ab-7

Eb/F D/E Db/Eb D-7

A/B Abmaj7/C Gmaj7/D Eb-11 Dmaj7#5/F# Cmaj7#5/G Absus2

C OUTRO-SOLO

REPEAT AND FADE

Eb-7 Ab-7 Eb-7 Ab-7 Eb-7 Ab-7 Eb-7

32-BAR AABA FORM, BEBOP LANGUAGE, ACCESSIBLE
FOR EARLY LEVEL IMPROVISATION, WITH SHIFT OF KEYS IN B SECTION.

ACCESSIBLE HARMONY, STANDARD AABA FORM.

PERDIDO

(MED. SWING)

DUKE ELLINGTON, THE CENTENNIAL COLLECTION: DUKE ELLINGTON, BMG MUSIC, 1972.

- HARRY LENK/ERVIN DRAKE/JUAN TIZOL

C-7 F7 Bb6

D-7 G7 C-7 F7

1. Bb6 Eb7 D-7 G7 2. Bb6 Eb7 Bb6

D7 3 G7

C7 3 F7

C-7 F7 Bb6 D-7 G7

C-7 F7 Bb6 Eb7 Bb6 (G7)

UNUSUAL DISPLACED RHYTHMS, SOPHISTICATED HARMONY.

POEM FOR #15 (THE SAGA OF HARRISON CRABFEATHERS)

MIKE MARSHALL & CHRIS THILE, INTO THE CAULDRON, SUGAR HILL RECORDS, 2003.

- STEPHEN L. KUHN

BLUESY BALLAD, ACCESSIBLE, SOMETIMES DONE WITH A 12/8 FEEL.

PLEASE SEND ME SOMEONE TO LOVE

GENE HARRIS, ALLEY CATS, CONCORD RECORDS, 2006.

(BALLAD)

- PERCY MAYFIELD

Ab7
A°7
Eb/Bb
G7/B
C7#9
F7
Ab/Bb
Bb7#9
C
Eb
Bb7#5
Eb7
Ab7
A°7
Eb/Bb
G7/B
C7#9
F7
Ab/Bb
TO
Eb
Eb7/G
Ab7
A°7
Eb/Bb
C7#9
F7
Bb7
D.S. AL, SOLOS OVER A
(TAKE REPEAT)
G7(#9 #5)
C7#9
F-7
G-7
Abmaj7
A°7
Ab/Bb
N.C.
Eb
Eb7/G
Ab7
A°7
Eb/Bb
E9
Eb9
RIT.

NICE INTERLUDE, HARMONICALLY ACCESSIBLE, AABA FORM.

POINCIANA
(SONG OF THE TREE)

(MED. LATIN)

AHMAD JAMAL, POINCIANA (LIVE), GEFFEN RECORDS, 1951.

- BUDDY BERNIER/NAT SIMON

A
Gmaj7
D-7
G7
C-7
Gmaj7 G6
Gmaj7 G6
B
C-7
Dmaj7
D6
C-7
A-7
D7
A
Gmaj7
D-7
G7
C-7
Gmaj7
(A-7 D7)

CLASSIC BALLAD, AABA FORM, BRIDGE MODULATES TO ANOTHER KEY.

POLKA DOTS AND MOONBEAMS

GOOD EXAMPLE OF MOTIVIC DEVELOPMENT AND SPECIAL FUNCTION DOMINANT (♭V I7).

POVO

(MED. JAZZ-FUNK)

FREDDIE HUBBARD, SKY DIVE, SONY/BMG MUSIC ENTERTAINMENT, 1972.

- FREDDIE HUBBARD

*A maj7#11 ON SOLOS

TECHNO/ROCK BLUES, WITH AMBIGUOUS KEY AREA IN THE BRIDGE, AND A DIRECT MODULATION UP A HALF STEP.
PRECIOUS
(MED.)
ANNIE LENNOX, DIVA, BMG ENTERTAINMENT INTERNATIONAL, 1992.
- ANNIE LENNOX
INTRO
N.C.
(BASS)
D-7
G-7
D-7
(BS. CONT. SIM.)
A
G-7
D-7
VERSE
D-7
G-7
D-7
A
G-7
D-7
1.

2.
A
G-7
D-7
BRIDGE
G-11
F
Bb
1.
Ebadd9
2.
Ebadd9
N.C.
TRUMPET SOLO
D-7
G-7
D-7
A
G-7
D-7
VERSE
Eb-7
Ab-7
Eb-7
OUTRO
Bb
Ab-7
Eb-7
REPEAT AND FADE

HARMONY (A THEME) INCLUDES SECONDARY DOMINANTS, SO YOU CAN VOICE LEAD INNER VOICES VERY CONCISELY BY STEP.

PRELUDE TO A KISS

(BALLAD)

BRAD MEHLDAU, INTRODUCING BRAD MEHLDAU, WARNER BROS., 1995.

– IRVING GORDON/IRVING MILLS/DUKE ELLINGTON

ED THIGPEN USES BRUSHES IN BOSSA NOVA AND LATIN JAZZ.

QUIET NIGHTS OF QUIET STARS
(CORCOVADO)

OSCAR PETERSON TRIO, WE GET REQUESTS, THE VERVE MUSIC GROUP, 1964.

(MED. BOSSA)

- GENE LEES/ANTONIO CARLOS JOBIM

BEBOP HEAD, AABA FORM.

RAY'S IDEA

MILES DAVIS, VOL. 2 (THE RUDY VAN GELDER EDITION REMASTERED), BLUE NOTE RECORDS, 2001 (1953).

(MED.)

- WALTER GIL FULLER/RAYMOND BROWN

FMAJ7 D-7 G-7 C7 A-7 D7 G-7 C7

C-7 F7 BbMAJ7 Eb7 1. G-7 C7 FMAJ7 C7

2. G-7 C7 FMAJ7 C-7 F7#5

Bb-7 Eb7#5 Ab-7 Db7#5

G-7 C7ALT FMAJ7 D-7

G-7 C7 A-7 D7 G-7 C7

C-7 F7 BbMAJ7 Eb7 G-7 C7 FMAJ7

MEDIUM TEMPO SWING TUNE.
ROBBINS NEST
(MED. SWING)
COUNT BASIE AND ELLA FITZGERALD, ELLA AND BASIE!, THE VERVE MUSIC GROUP, 1963.
- SIR CHARLES THOMPSON/ILLINOIS JACQUET
C6
Ab7
E-7
Ebo7
D-7
G7
C6
Ebo7
D-7
G7
C6
Db6
C6
E7
A7
D7
G7
D-7
G7
C6
Ab7
E-7
Ebo7
D-7
G7
C6
Db6
C6

(BALLAD)

'ROUND MIDNIGHT

- THELONIOUS MONK/COOTIE WILLIAMS/BERNIE HANIGHEN

GOOD JAM-BAND BLUES TUNE.
THE SAD NITE OWL
FREDDY KING, JUST PICKIN', MODERN BLUES, 1990.
(MED. BLUES)
- SONNY THOMPSON
A
G
C
G
(GUITARS)
C
G
D
TO
C
G
D7#5
B GUITAR SOLO
G9
C9
G9
C9
G9
Ab9
G9
D9
C9
G9
Ab9
G9
D7
D.S. AL
C
G

ST. THOMAS

(CALYPSO)

- SONNY ROLLINS

C6 E-7 A7 D-7 G7 C6

C6 E-7 A7 D-7 G7 C6

E-7b5 Bb7 A7 D-7 A7#5 G7

C6 C7/E F6 F#o7 C6/E G7 C6

REPEAT HEAD IN/OUT

GREAT BRUSH WORK, AABA FORM, STRAIGHT AHEAD, GOOD FOR LEARNING IMPROVISATION. FOR DRUMMERS, ILLUSTRATES GREAT USE OF THE "CONVENTIONAL STROKE," ALONG WITH ACCENT APPLICATION, AND TASTEFUL SPARSE FILLS.

SATIN DOLL

DUKE ELLINGTON AND ELLA FITZGERALD, COTE D'AZUR CONCERTS ON VERVE, UMG RECORDINGS, INC., 1966.

(MED.)

- DUKE ELLINGTON

GOOD JAM-BAND TUNE.

SAN-HO-ZAY

(MED.)

LET'S HIDE AWAY AND DANCE AWAY, GUSTO RECORDS, INC. BLUES, 1991 (1964).

- FREDDY KING/SONNY THOMPSON

A W/AD LIB. THROUGHOUT ON REPEATS

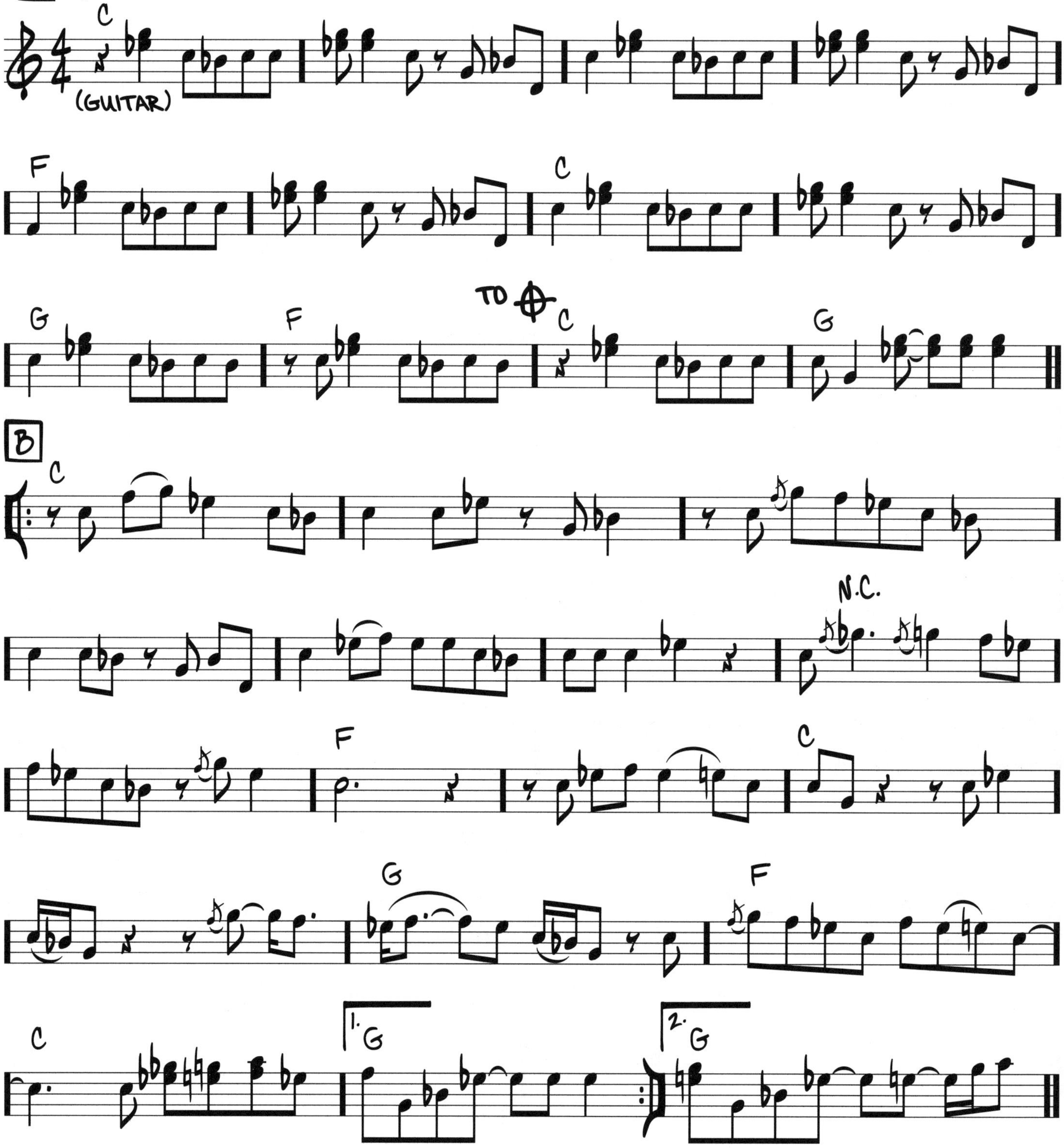
C
(GUITAR)
F
C
G
F
TO ⊕
C
G
B
C
N.C.
F
C
G
F
C
1. G
2. G

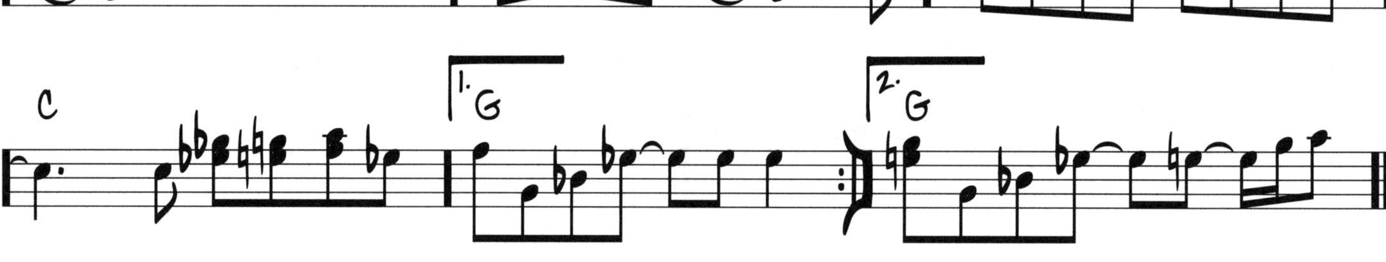

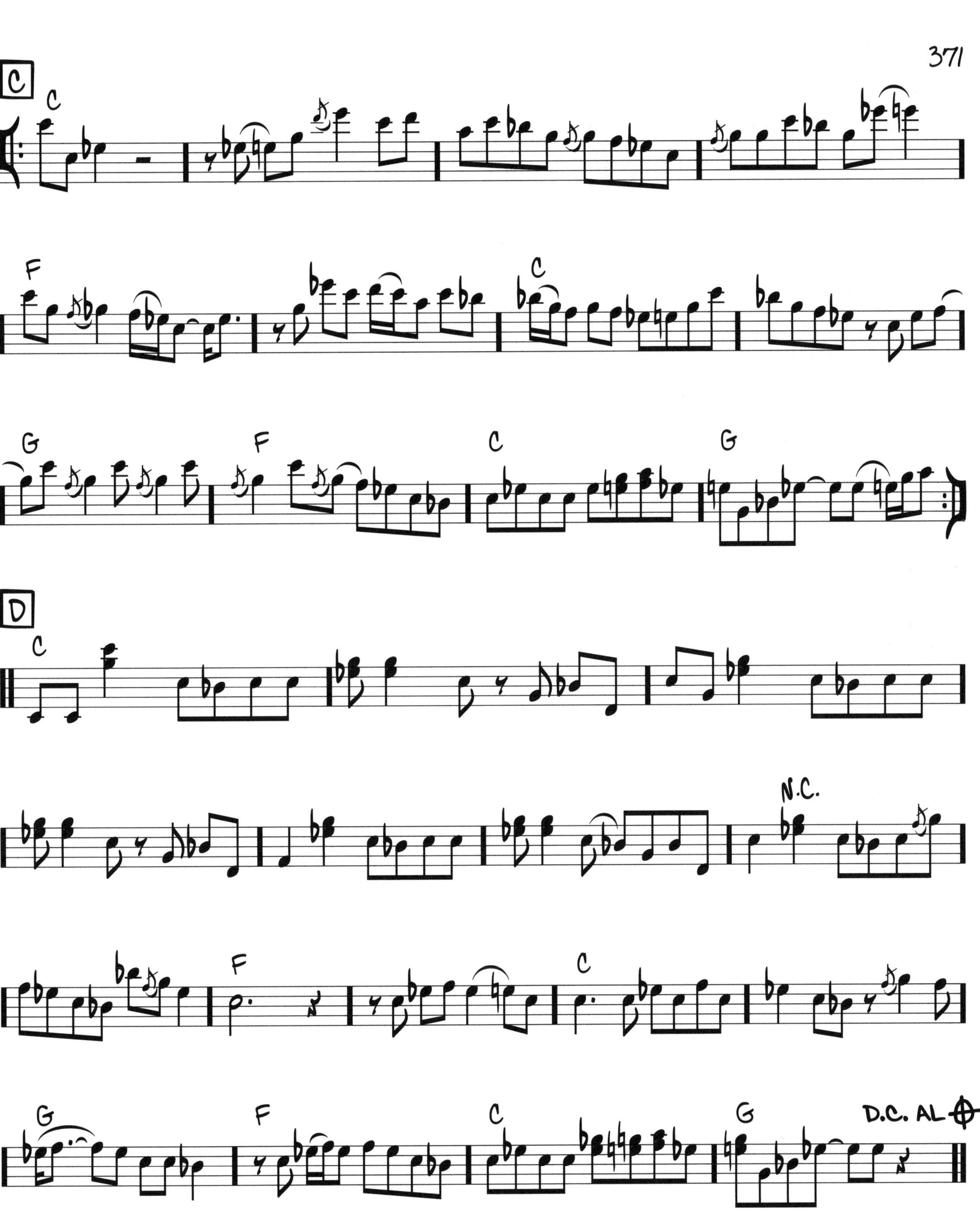
C
C
F
C
G
F
C
G
D
C
N.C.
F
C
G
F
C
G
D.C. AL
C
N.C.
Db9
C9

BEBOP, BASED ON "HONEYSUCKLE ROSE," STRAIGHT-AHEAD, HARD-CORE BEBOP WITH AABA FORM AND HARMONY.

(SOUL JAZZ)
SIDEWINDER
- LEE MORGAN
D7
Eb7
BASS & RHYTHM - CONTINUE SIMILE
(Ab7) G7
Ab7
(Eb7) D7
Eb7
G-7b5
C7b9
F-
G-/C
F-/Bb
Eb7
(Eb7) D7
Eb7
Eb7
N.C.
PLAY HEAD 2X IN/OUT
(ENDING)
D7
Eb7
VAMP TO FADE OR CUE

GREAT GROOVE/DANCE TUNE.

SERPENTINE FIRE

ALL 'N' ALL, SONY MUSIC ENTERTAINMENT, INC., 1977.

(MED. FUNK)

- MAURICE WHITE/VERDINE WHITE/REGINALD BURKE

INTRO

D- E- G13sus4 D- E- A7(#9 #5) D- E- G13sus4

C-7

VERSE

C-7

8VA

CHORUS
C-7
8VA
8VA
C
D-/C
C
D-/A
C/G
D-/G
C
D-/C
C
TO
D-/A
C/G
D-/G
C
C-7
D.S. AL
D-/A
C/G
D-/G
C
C-7
8VA TILL END
OUTRO-CHORUS
C-7
REPEAT AND FADE

GOOD JAM-BAND TUNE.
SIDE TRACKED
(MED. BLUES)
LET'S HIDE AWAY AND DANCE AWAY, GUSTO RECORDS, INC. BLUES, 1991 (1964).
- FREDDIE KING/SONY THOMPSON
INTRO
D7 C7 G7 D7
(GUITAR)
A
AD LIB. THROUGHOUT ON REPEATS
G7 C7 G7
C7
G7 D7
C7 G7
1.
2.
B
C7 G7 C7 G7
C7 G7 A7 D7
C
G7 C7 G7

C7
G7
TO
D7
C7
G7
D7
D
G7
C7
G7
C7
G7
LAST X, D.S. AL
D7
C7
G7
D7
D7
C7
G7
Ab9
G9

MELODIC MINOR SCALE IN OPENING MELODY AND AS CHORD SOURCE, TRIAD INVERSIONS, GUIDE TONE LINE ON BRIDGE (1 7 b7 6), MODULATIONS.

SISTER MOON

STING, NOTHING LIKE THE SUN, UMG RECORDINGS, 1987.

(MED. SLOW)

- STING

INTRO/SAX SOLO

F#-(maj9) B7 F#-(maj9) B7 F#-(maj9) B7 F#-(maj9) B7

(BASS)

VERSE

D#-7b5 E/G# F#-/C# F#-(maj9) B7 F#-(maj9) B7

F#-(maj9) B7 F#-(maj9) B7

BRIDGE

Bb- Bb-(maj7)/F

Bb-7 Bb-6/F Bb- Bb-(maj7)/F

Bb-7 Bb-6/F Eb-7 F-7

Gb-7 Cb D#-7b5 E/G# F#-/C#

D#-7 G#7 D#-7b5 E/G# F#-/C#

F#-(maj9) B7 F#-(maj9) B7 F#-(maj9) B7 F#-(maj9) B7

OUTRO/SAX SOLO

REPEAT AND FADE

F#-(maj9) B7 F#-(maj9) B7 F#-(maj9) B7 F#-(maj9) B7

BALLAD, GOOD FOR PLAYING VERY SLOWLY.
SO AMAZING
(MED. SLOW)
GIVE ME THE REASON, SONY MUSIC ENTERTAINMENT, 1986.
- LUTHER VANDROSS
INTRO
B6
(GUITAR)
C♯/D♯
VERSE
B
G♯-7
D♯-7
Emaj7
D♯-7
C♯-7
CONT. SIM.
E/F♯
B
G♯-7
D♯-7
Emaj7
D♯-7
C♯-7
E/F♯
Emaj7
F♯7
E/F♯
B
G♯-7
D♯-7
Emaj7
D♯-7
C♯-7
1. C♯/D♯
2. C♯/D♯

BRIDGE
D#-7 Emaj7 D#-7 C#-7 E/F#
Emaj7 D#-7 Emaj7 C#/D#
D#-7 Emaj7 D#-7 C#-7 E/F# Emaj7 D#-7
Emaj7 C#/D#
VERSE
C# A#-7
E#-7 F#maj7 E#-7 D#-7 F#/G#
F#maj7 G#7 F#/G# C# A#-7 E#-7 F#maj7
OUTRO
F#/G# F#maj7 G#7 F#/G#
C# A#-7 E#-7 F#maj7
REPEAT AND FADE

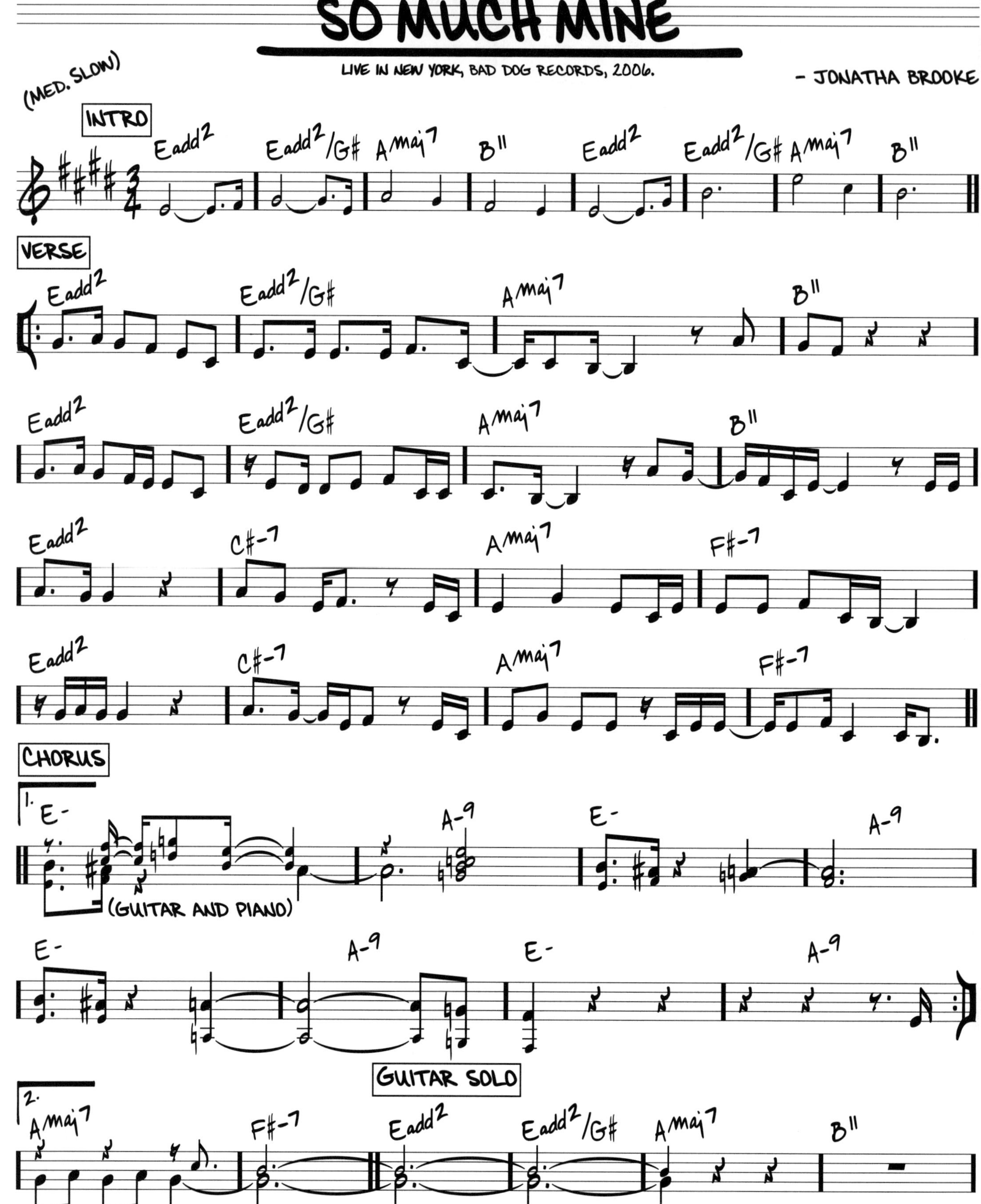
MOSTLY DIATONIC HARMONY VERSES, FIRST INVERSION TRIADS, V7SUS4, ACCIDENTALS, AND 2-PART VOCAL HARMONY.
SO MUCH MINE
LIVE IN NEW YORK, BAD DOG RECORDS, 2006.
- JONATHA BROOKE
(MED. SLOW)
INTRO
Eadd2
Eadd2/G#
Amaj7
B11
VERSE
C#-7
F#-7
CHORUS
E-
A-9
(GUITAR AND PIANO)
GUITAR SOLO

Eadd2 Eadd2/G# Amaj7 B11 Eadd2 C#-7 Amaj7 F#-7

E- A-9 E- A-9

VERSE

Eadd2 Eadd2/G# Amaj7 B11

Eadd2 Eadd2/G# Amaj7 B11

Eadd2 Eadd2/G# Amaj7 F#-7

Eadd2 C#-7 1. Amaj7

2. Amaj7 F#-7 Amaj7 F#-7

OUTRO-CHORUS

E- A-9 E- A-9

E- A-9 E- A-9 E5

CLASSIC MODAL TUNE, STANDARD AABA FORM, WITH THE B SECTION UP HALF A STEP.
SO WHAT
(MED. JAZZ)
MILES DAVIS, KIND OF BLUE, SONY, 1959 (1957).
- MILES DAVIS
A
N.C.
E-7add11
D-7add11
(BASS LINE MELODY 8VA)
1.
2.
B
F-7add11
Eb-7add11

N.C.
F-7add11
Eb-7add11
N.C.
N.C.
F-7add11
Eb-7add11
N.C.
N.C.
F-7add11
Eb-7add11
N.C.
A
N.C.
E-7add11
D-7add11
N.C.
E-7add11
D-7add11
N.C.
E-7add11
D-7add11
N.C.
E-7add11
D-7add11
SOLOS
N.C.
D-7
16
Eb-7
8
D-7
8
AFTER SOLOS, PLAY ENTIRE FORM
THEN VAMP ON A - FADE OR CUE

A GREAT TUNE FOR IMPROVISING FROM MINOR TO THE RELATIVE MAJOR KEY.

SOFTLY AS IN A MORNING SUNRISE

BASED ON CHORD PROGRESSIONS FROM THE JAZZ STANDARDS REPERTOIRE.

SOLAR

MILES DAVIS ALL STARS, WALKIN', CONCORD MUSIC GROUP, 1954.

- MILES DAVIS

SOME PEOPLE'S LIVES

JANIS IAN, BREAKING SILENCE, MORGAN CREEK, 1993.

(BALLAD)

- RHONDA FLEMING/JANIS IAN

1
Csus2
Csus2/Bb
A-
Gsus4
G
D.S.S. AL 2
2
C
G
G/F
E7
E7/G#
A-
D
D7/F#
Gsus4
G
D
Csus2
Csus2/Bb
A-
Gsus2
G
E
F
Gsus4 G
F
Gsus4 G
F
G
G/F
E-7
A-
A-/G
RIT.
Fadd9
G
Cadd9

SIMPLE, STRAIGHT-AHEAD SWING TUNE, ABAB FORM.

SOMETIMES I'M HAPPY

(MED.)

SARAH VAUGHAN, SARAH VAUGHAN AT MISTER KELLY'S (LIVE 1957), UMG RECORDINGS, 1957.

- CLIFFORD GREY/IRVING CAESAR/VINCENT YOUMANS

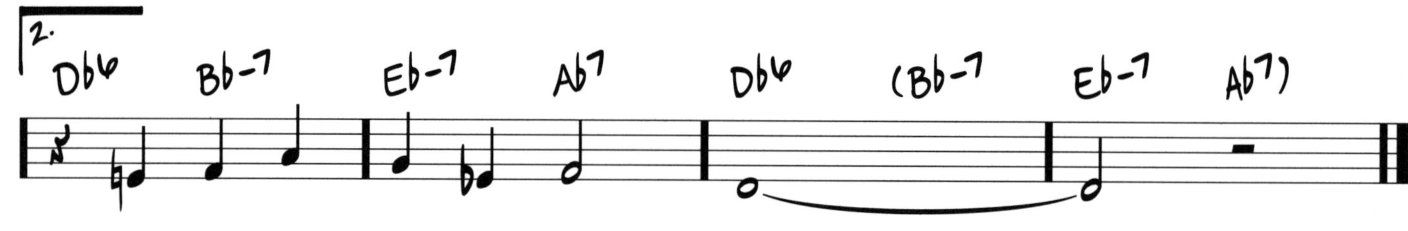

GOOD JAM-BAND TUNE, EXAMPLE OF NEW ORLEANS FUNK.
SOPHISTICATED CISSY
(MED. SLOW FUNK)
THE METERS, WARNER BROS. RECORDS, 1969.
- ARTHUR NEVILLE/LEO NOCENTELLI/
GEORGE PORTER, JR./JOSEPH MODELISTE, JR.
INTRO
C
D-
(GUITAR)
A
ORGAN THEME
AD LIB. THROUGHOUT ON REPEATS
C9
(ORGAN)
(GUITAR)
B
GUITAR THEME
D-7
A-7
C
ORGAN SOLO/OUTRO
REPEAT AND FADE

A MODERN JAZZ CLASSIC OFFERING LESS TRADITIONAL HARMONIC APPROACHES FOR IMPROVISING.

THE SORCERER

(FAST JAZZ)

HERBIE HANCOCK, SPEAK LIKE A CHILD, BLUE NOTE RECORDS, 2005.

- HERBIE HANCOCK

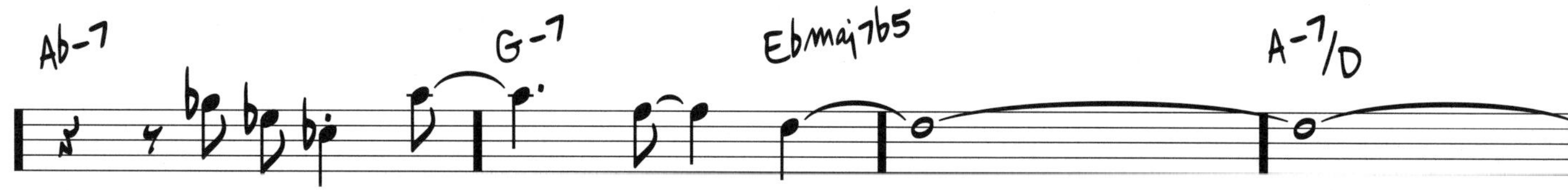

HAUNTING BALLAD WITH RICH HARMONIES.
(BALLAD)
SOUL EYES
JOHN COLTRANE, COLTRANE (IMPULSE!), UMG RECORDINGS, 1962.
- MAL WALDRON
C-7 G7b9 C-7 F7
F-7 Bb7#9 G-7b5 C7b9
Abmaj7 A-7b5 D7b9 Gmaj7 Ab-7 Db7
Gbmaj7 F-7 Bb7 Ebmaj7 D-7b5 G7b9
C-7 G7b9 C-7 F7
F-7 Bb7#9 G-7b5 C7b9
Abmaj7 A-7b5 D7b9 G-7b5 C7b9
F-7 Bb7#9 Ebmaj7 (D-7b5 G7b9)

GREAT HORN LINES.

SOUL MAN

SAM AND DAVE, STAX/ATLANTIC RECORDS, 1967.

- ISAAC HAYES/DAVID PORTER

F
G
1., 2.
C
D
N.C.
(HORNS)
3.
C
D
N.C.
(HORNS)
BRIDGE
Eb
Bb
C
C/D
Db/Eb
INTERLUDE
Ab
(GUITAR)
Gb
Cb
Db
Eb
OUTRO-CHORUS
Ab
Bb- Ab
Bb- Ab
Bb- Ab
REPEAT AND FADE
Bb- Ab

CHALLENGING RHYTHMS, FUSION FEEL, INTERESTING INTERLUDES, RELATIVELY ADVANCED, SPANISH SCALE FLAVOR (MAJOR AND MINOR THIRDS).

G maj7
C#7
F#7
B-
B7
D
E-7
A7
D maj7
C#7
F#7
LAST X, D.S.S. AL ⊕
E
B sus4
B add9
N.C.
F
SOLO
G maj7
F#7
E-7
A7
D maj7
G maj7
C#7
F#7
B-
B7
OPEN
LAST X
G maj7
D.S.
G maj7
D/Bb
B sus4

A SHORTER CLASSIC THAT HAS AN ASYMMETRICAL, NON-32-BAR AABA FORM.
(MED. SWING)
SPEAK NO EVIL
WAYNE SHORTER, SPEAK NO EVIL, BLUE NOTE RECORDS, 1999 (1964).
- WAYNE SHORTER
TO
AFTER SOLOS, D.S. AL
(PLAY PICKUPS)
REPEAT TILL END

SPOONFUL

(MED. SHUFFLE)
INTRO
- WILLIE DIXON
E7
(GUITAR)
VERSE
E7
CHORUS
E7
3
(W/ INTRO RIFF)
1.
2.,3.
TO
SOLO
D.S. AL
OUTRO
REPEAT & FADE
E7
5
[SOLO OVER E7]

EXAMPLE OF MODAL INTERCHANGE, MODULATIONS, INCOMPLETE CHORDS.

SPECIAL

JANET JACKSON, THE VELVET ROPE, VIRGIN RECORDS AMERICA, 1997.

- JAMES HARRIS III/TERRY LEWIS/JANET JACKSON

CHORUS

C G/B A-7 C/D

C G/B A-7 C/D

C G/B G-/Bb A7

C/D N.C. G-9 Abmaj7 TO ⊕

Ebmaj9 C-9 G-9 Abmaj7 Ebmaj9 C-9

BRIDGE

G-9 Abmaj7 Ebmaj9 C-9

G-9 Abmaj7 Ebmaj9 C-9 G-9 Abmaj7

3

Ebmaj9 C-9 G-9 Abmaj7 Ebmaj9 C-9 D.S. AL ⊕

6

⊕

Ebmaj9 C-9 N.C.

BALLAD, RELATIVELY DIFFICULT, AABA' FORM, HARMONICALLY SOPHISTICATED.

SPRING CAN REALLY HANG YOU UP THE MOST

ELLA FITZGERALD, CLAP HANDS, HERE COMES CHARLIE!, THE VERVE MUSIC GROUP, 1961.

- FRAN LANDESMAN/TOMMY WOLF

Eb-7 Abmaj7 Ab-7 Dbmaj7 Ab-7 Dbmaj7
D-7 G7 F-7 Bb7 Ebmaj7 Dbmaj7
3
Abmaj7 Gbmaj7 Abmaj7 F-7 Bb-7 Eb7 C-7b5 F7
Dbmaj7 Gb7#11 TO ⊕ Ab/C E7#11 Bb-7 Eb7
C-7 B7 Bb-7 A7#11
AFTER SOLOS, D.S. AL ⊕
(TAKE REPEAT)
⊕ B-7 E7 Bb-7 Eb7
C-7b5 F7 Bb-7/Eb Abmaj7/Eb Bb-7/Eb Abmaj7/Eb
G-7b5 C7b9 F-7 Bb7 Bb-7 Gb7
C-7 F7 Bb-7 Amaj7 Abmaj7
RIT.

SOPHISTICATED HARMONICALLY, ABA FORM.

STAR EYES
(BOSSA NOVA)
- DON RAYE/GENE DePAUL
F6 G-7 C7 F6 F-7 Bb7
Eb6 A-7b5 D7(b13 b9) G6/9 Db7 C7
Bbmaj9 Bb-7 Eb13#11
Abmaj7 G-7 C7sus4 C7b9
F6 G-7 C7 F6 F-7 Bb7
Eb6 A-7b5 D7(b13 b9) G6/9 G-7b5 C13 C7b13
F6 Eb7 D7#9 G-7 C7sus4 F6
3

VERY INTERESTING VERSE. ABAC FORM, DIATONIC AND SECONDARY DOMINANTS.

STARDUST

NATALIE COLE, STARDUST, ELEKTRA/WEA, 1996.

(MED. BALLAD)

- MITCHELL PARISH/HOAGY CARMICHAEL

RICH HARMONIES, FAVORED BY JAZZ PLAYERS.

STELLA BY STARLIGHT

(MED. OR BALLAD)

MILES DAVIS, MILES IN BERLIN, COLUMBIA, 1964.

- NED WASHINGTON/VICTOR YOUNG

E-7b5 A7b9 C-7 F7

F-7 Bb7 Ebmaj7 Ab7

Bbmaj7 E-7b5 A7b9 D-7 Bb-7 Eb7

Fmaj7 E-7b5 A7b9 A-7b5 D7b9

G7#5 C-7

3

Ab7#11 Bbmaj7

E-7b5 A7b9 D-7b5 G7b9

C-7b5 F7b9 Bbmaj7

VERSES DEVELOP TO CAUSE THE CHORUS TO GAIN MORE WEIGHT EACH TIME WE HEAR IT.

TO 𝄌

Ebadd9 C-(add9) Fadd9 G-7

VERSE

G- Eb/G

A7 Dsus4 D C-(add9)

F G- E-7b5

C-(add9) Dsus4 D D.S. AL 𝄌 𝄌 Fadd9

BRIDGE

E-9 Csus2 Asus2

Gsus2 C-9 Abadd9 Bbadd9 F6

OUTRO-CHORUS

E-(add9) Cadd9 A-7 Dsus4 D

E-(add9) Cadd9 A-(add9) Dadd9 E-(add9) Cadd9

A-(add9) Dadd9 Cadd9 Dadd9 REPEAT AND FADE

STOLEN MOMENTS

(MED. SWING)

- OLIVER NELSON

A 12-BAR BLUES BUT WITH ♭II9, CHROMATIC MINOR 7'S, HYBRID VOICINGS OF V7 AND ♭VI.

(SLOW BLUES)

(THEY CALL IT) STORMY MONDAY

(STORMY MONDAY BLUES)

THE ALLMAN BROTHERS BAND, THE ALLMAN BROTHERS BAND AT FILLMORE EAST, THE ISLAND DEF JAM MUSIC GROUP, 1969.

- AARON "T-BONE" WALKER

STRAIGHTEN UP AND FLY RIGHT

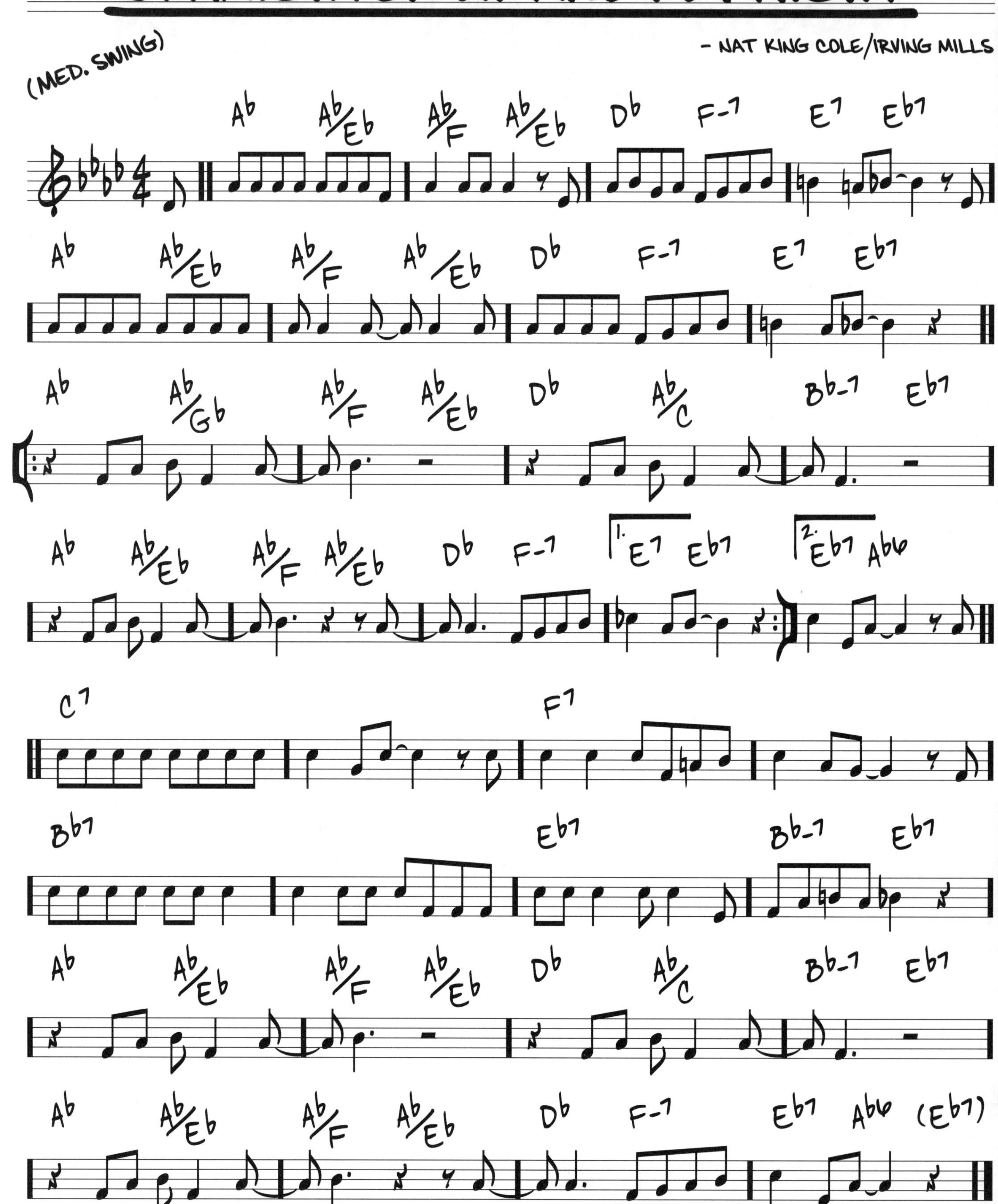

ONE OF THE LANDMARK RECORDINGS IN THE HISTORY OF JAZZ.

STRUTTIN' WITH SOME BARBECUE

LOUIS ARMSTRONG AND HIS HOT FIVES AND SEVENS VOLUME III, CBS RECORDS, 1989 (1927).

- LILLIAN HARDIN ARMSTRONG/DON RAYE

DOUBLING MELODIC RHYTHM TO CREATE PRESSURE AND SUPPORT THE INTENSIFYING LYRIC.
STRAWBERRY WINE
(MED.)
DEANA CARTER, DID I SHAVE MY LEGS FOR THIS?, CAPITOL RECORDS NASHVILLE, 1996.
- MATRACA BERG/GARY HARRISON
INTRO
Db
Gb
(PEDAL STEEL)
VERSE
Db
Gb
Db
Ab
Db
Gb
Db
Ab
PRE-CHORUS
Db/F
Gb
Db/F
Gb
Ab
Gb
Ab
Gb
CHORUS
Db
Ab/C
Bb-
Gb

Db
Ab
Bb-
Gb
Db
1.
Gb
2.
BRIDGE
Eb-6
Eb-7
Eb-6
Eb-7
Bb-
Db
Ab/C
Ab
N.C.
PEDAL STEEL SOLO
Db
Ab/C
Bb-
Gb
OUTRO-CHORUS
3rd X, GUITAR SOLO
Db
Ab/C
Bb-
Gb
Db
Ab
Bb-
Gb
REPEAT AND FADE

GOOD JAM-BAND TUNE.

THE STUMBLE

FREDDY KING, LET'S HIDE AWAY AND DANCE AWAY, GUSTO RECORDS, INC., 1991 (1964).

E7/B
C♯7
F♯7
B7
E7
A7
E7
2.
E7
A7
A♯o7
E7/B
C♯7
F♯7
B7
E7
A7
E7
C
A7
E7
A7
B7
E7 N.C.
E7 N.C.
A7 N.C.
A7 N.C.
A♯o7
E7/B
C♯7
F♯7
B7
1. E7
A7
E7
2. E7
A7
E7

MINOR-BLUES CLASSIC, NICELY CONSTRUCTED PENTATONIC MELODY.

EARLY SIXTIES SOUL CLASSIC, WITH BLUESY MINOR FEEL.

SUNNY

SUNNY, THE ISLAND DEF JAM MUSIC GROUP, 1966.

(MED. ROCK)

- BOBBY HEBB

A- | C7 | FMaj7 |
B-7 E7 | A- | C7 |
FMaj7 | B-7 E7 | A- |
C7 | FMaj7 | Bb7#11 |
B-7 E7 | TO ⊕ A- | B-7b5 E7 AFTER SOLOS, D.C. AL ⊕

⊕

A- (LAST X) | B-7b5 E7 |

SWEET HOME CHICAGO

VERSE
E7
A7
E7
3
B7
3
A7
1.-3.
4.
E
E7/D
E°7/Db
A-/C
E7/B
B7
E7/B
B7
E7

CHALLENGING VOCALLY. GOOD FOR VOCALISTS TO LISTEN TO GUITAR PATTERNS AND RHYTHM MODULATIONS. INSTRUMENTALISTS, DON'T RUSH ACCOMPANIMENT PATTERNS!

SWEET THING
(SWEET THANG)

1. Amaj7 Dmaj7 Amaj7 Dmaj7 Amaj7 Dmaj7 Amaj7 Dmaj7

2. Amaj7 Dmaj7 Amaj7 Dmaj7 Amaj7 Dmaj7 Amaj7 Dmaj7

INTERLUDE

Bbmaj7 Ebmaj7 Bbmaj7 Ebmaj7 Bbmaj7 Ebmaj7 Bbmaj7 Ebmaj7

(GUITAR)

VERSE

Bbmaj7 Ebmaj7 Bbmaj7 Ebmaj7

Bbmaj7 Ebmaj7 Bbmaj7 Ebmaj7

Bbmaj7 Ebmaj7 Bbmaj7 Ebmaj7

Bbmaj7 Ebmaj7 D-7 Db7#11 C-7 B7#11

OUTRO

Bbmaj7 Ebmaj7 Bbmaj7 Emaj7

REPEAT AND FADE

Bbmaj7 Ebmaj7 D-7 Db7#11 C-7 B7#11

VERSE MELODY IS AN EXCELLENT EXAMPLE OF AN UNSTABLE PHRASE RESOLVING TO A STABLE PHRASE.

SWEETNESS FOLLOWS

R.E.M., AUTOMATIC FOR THE PEOPLE, WARNER BROS./WEA, 1992.

- BILL BERRY/PETER BUCK/MIKE MILLS/MICHAEL STIPE

CHORUS
Bbadd9/F Cadd9/G Bbadd9/F Cadd9/G
D E-11/D D E-11/D Bbadd9/F Cadd9/G
D.S. AL
Bbadd9/F Cadd9/G D E-11/D D E-11/D
INTERLUDE
A/D Gadd2/D A/D Gadd2/D
CHORUS
D E-11/D D E-11/D Bbadd9/F Cadd9/G
Bbadd9/F Cadd9/G D E-11/D D E-11/D
Bbadd9/F Cadd9/G Bbadd9/F Cadd9/G D E-11/D
OUTRO
D E-11/D D E-11/D D
PLAY 6X

ICONIC TUNE, AABA FORM, MAKES USE OF WHOLE TONE SCALE IN THE SECOND CHORD.
TAKE THE "A" TRAIN
(MED.)
DUKE ELLINGTON, REMINISCING IN TEMPO, SONY, 1991.
- BILLY STRAYHORN
C6
D7#11
D-7
G7
C6
1.
D-7
G7
2.
G-7
C7
FMaj7
D7
D-7
G7
G7b9
C6
D7#11
D-7
G7
TO
C6
D-7
G7
AFTER SOLOS, D.C. AL
(TAKE REPEAT)
C6
N.C.
CMaj7

BLUESY POP BALLAD, AABA FORM, ACCESSIBLE.
TEACH ME TONIGHT
(MED. SLOW SWING)
AL JARREAU, BREAKIN' AWAY, WARNER BROS. RECORDS, 1970.
- SAMMY CAHN/GENE DEPAUL
Gb/Ab Dbmaj7 F-7 Bb7b9
Eb-7 F-7b5 Bb7b9 Eb-7
1. Gb/Ab Ab7b9 Dbmaj7 Bb-7 Gb/Ab
2. Gb/Ab Ab7b9
Db6 Gb13 Dbmaj7 Eo7 Eb-7 Ab7 F-7 Bb7b9
Eb-7 Ab7 Dbmaj7 G-7b5 C7b9 F-7
Bb-7 Eb7 Gb/Ab Dbmaj7
F-7 Bb7b9 Eb-7 F-7b5 Bb7b9
Eb-7 Gb/Ab Ab7b9 Db6 (Gb13 Dbmaj7 Gb/Ab)

MODAL INTERCHANGE, SECONDARY DOMINANTS.

TAKIN' IT TO THE STREETS

THE DOOBIE BROTHERS, TAKIN' IT TO THE STREETS, WARNER BROS., 1976.

- MICHAEL McDONALD

C5 C5/Bb F/A F-/Ab F/G TO ⊕

C7/E F F-/F# C/G F/G C7/E F F-/F# C/G F/G

C7/E F F-/F# C/G F/G C7/E F F-/F# C/G

F/G C7/E F F-/F# C/G F/G PLAY 3X

C7/E F F-/F# C/G SOLO F/G C/G

D7/G G7sus4 1., 2., 3. 4. D.S. AL ⊕

⊕ OUTRO-CHORUS

C7/E F F-/F# C/G REPEAT AND FADE F/G

EXAMPLE OF 2-PART AND 3-PART VOCAL HARMONY.

TEACH YOUR CHILDREN

CROSBY, STILLS, NASH, & YOUNG, DEJA VU, ATLANTA RECORDING CORPORATION, 1970.

- GRAHAM NASH

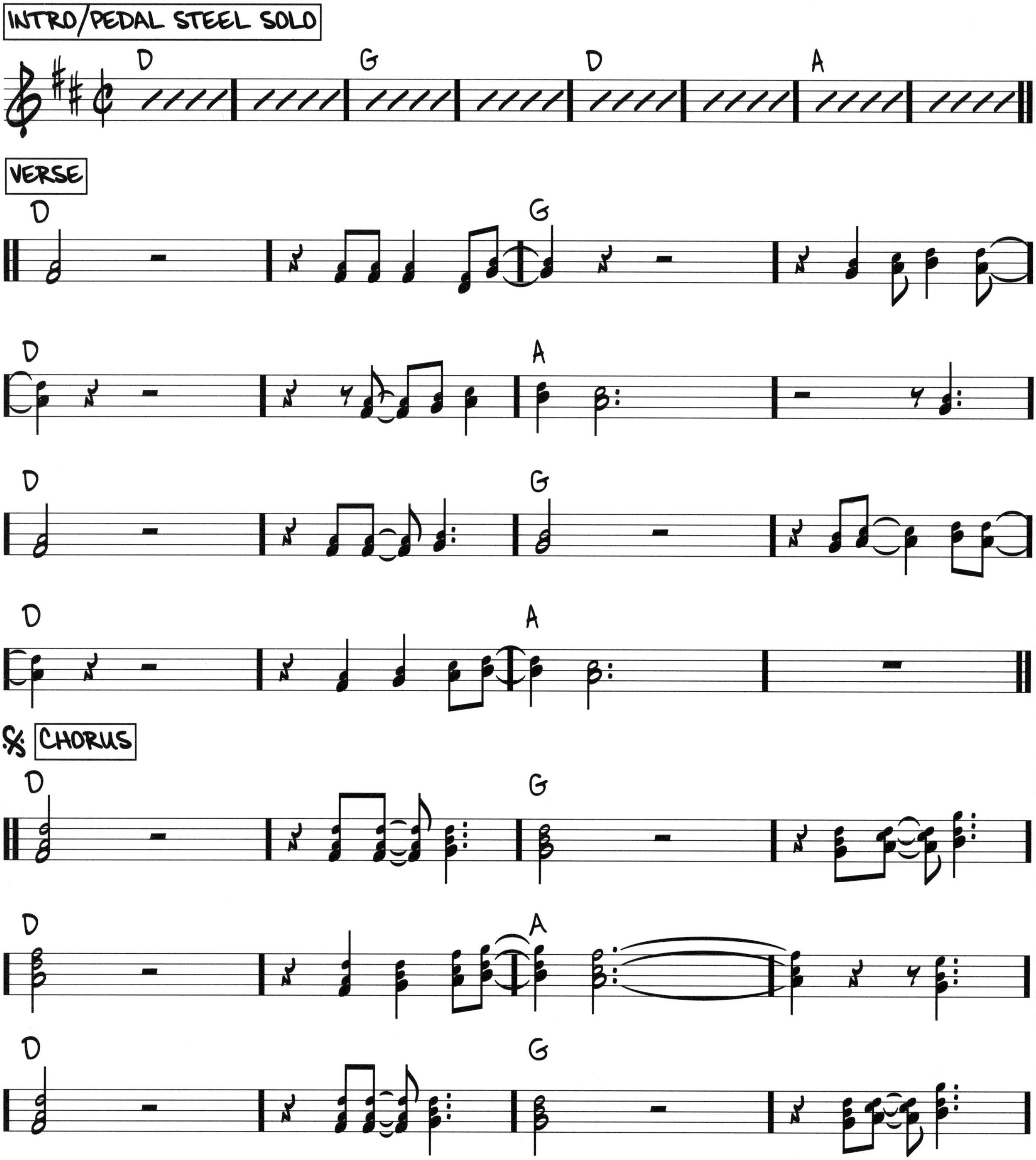

INTRO/PEDAL STEEL SOLO

D G D A

VERSE

D G

D A

D G

D A

CHORUS

D G

D A

D G

D
A
D
G
D
B-
G
A
D
TO
PEDAL STEEL SOLO
G
D
A
VERSE
D
G
D
A
D
G
D
A
D.S. AL
OUTRO/PEDAL STEEL SOLO
G
D
A
D
A D

SEQUENTIAL MELODY MOVES BACK AND FORTH FROM MAJOR TO MINOR.

TENDERLY

NAT KING COLE, THE UNFORGETTABLE NAT KING COLE, CAPITOL RECORDS, 1999.

(MED. BALLAD)

- JACK LAWRENCE/WALTER GROSS

GOOD EXAMPLE OF A SLOW BLUES (12/8).

TEXAS FLOOD

(SLOW BLUES)

STEVIE RAY VAUGHAN & DOUBLE TROUBLE, TEXAS FLOOD, SONY/BMG MUSIC ENTERTAINMEN., 1983.

- LARRY DAVIS/JOSEPH W. SCOTT

INTRO-SOLO

G A-/C G C D-/C C G7 D7

SOLO

G7 C7 G7 C7

G7 D7 C7 G7 C7 G D7

VERSE

G7 C7 G7

C7 G7

D7 TO ⊕ C7 G7 C7 1. G7 D7

2. G7 D7 SOLO 1. G7 D7 2. G7 D7

⊕

C7 N.C. G7 C7 G7 F#7 G7 G7/B

MODAL INTERCHANGE, 7TH CHORD INVERSIONS, GUIDE TONE LINES, SUBSTITUTE DOMINANTS.

THAT LOOK YOU WEAR
(ESTE SEU OLHAR)

(MED. BOSSA)

ZOOT SIMS, JIMMY DRANEY & JIM HALL, TWO JIMS AND ZOOT, MAINSTREAM RECORDS, 1964.

- GENE LEES/ANTONIO CARLOS JOBIM

CLASSIC 32-BAR FORM WITH TWO 16-BAR PHRASES.

THERE WILL NEVER BE ANOTHER YOU

SONNY ROLLINS, THE ESSENTIAL SONNY ROLLINS: THE RCA YEARS, RCA, 1962.

(UP)

- MACK GORDON/HARRY WARREN

Ebmaj7 D-7b5 G7

C-7 Bb-7 Eb7

Abmaj7 Db7 Ebmaj7 C-7

F7 F-7 Bb7

Ebmaj7 D-7b5 G7

C-7 Bb-7 Eb7

Abmaj7 Db9 Ebmaj7 A-7 D7

Ebmaj7 Ab7#11 Eb6/G C7 F-7 Bb7 Eb6 (Bb7)

FINE

MODAL INTERCHANGE, HYBRID VOICINGS OF BACKGROUND VOCALS, DECEPTIVE RESOLUTION.

BRIDGE
G# C#maj7 C#-7 F#7 D#-7
G# C#-7 F#7sus4 A#-7
VERSE
D#7 F#7sus4 E-6 G#-
C#-7 F#7sus4 E-6 A7 D
B-7 F#-7 E/F# F#7
CHORUS
Emaj7 B/D# B-/D
C#-7 F#7sus4 Emaj9 B/D#
OUTRO
B-/D 1. Gmaj7 F#7sus4 2. Gmaj7 F#7sus4 Badd9 E-6/B
Badd9 E-6/B Badd9 E-6/B Badd9
RIT.

MINOR PENTATONIC MELODY, 12-BAR BLUES, bVIMAJ7.

THE THRILL IS GONE

(SLOW, FUNKY)

B.B. KING, BLUES IS KING, CAPITOL RECORDS NASHVILLE, 1996.

- ROY HAWKINS/RICK DARNELL

INTRO/SOLO

B- E-

B- Gmaj7 F#7 B-

VERSE

B-

E- B-

Gmaj7 F#7 1. B-

2. B-7

SOLO (INTRO CHORDS) 10 (B-) TO ⊕ AFTER SOLOS, D.S. AL ⊕

⊕ B- REPEAT AND FADE

CHORD PATTERN MOTION, SUCH AS I VI II V, FUN FOR IMPROVISING.

EXAMPLE OF MULTIPLE TONICIZATIONS (SHORT MODULATIONS).

THROUGH THE FIRE

(SLOW)

CHAKA KHAN, I FEEL FOR YOU, RHINO/WARNER BROS. 2006.

- DAVID FOSTER/TOM KEANE/CYNTHIA WEIL

CHORUS
F-7 Bb-7 Eb/G
Ab C-7 Dbmaj7 G-7 C7b9
F-7 Bb-7 Eb/G
Ab C-7 Dbmaj7 G-7 C7#5
Dbmaj9 Dbmaj7/Eb TO
1. Abmaj9 Eb/Db Cbmaj7 Db/Eb
W/INTRO RIFF
2. Ab Db-7 Abmaj7 Db-7
AD LIB.
C-7 F-7 Bb-7 C-7 Dbmaj9 Db/Eb
D.S. AL
Db/Eb F-7 Bb-7 Db/Eb F-7
OUTRO
Bb-7 Db/Eb F-7 Bb-7 Db/Eb F-7
REPEAT AND FADE

MODAL INTERCHANGE, MIXOLYDIAN MELODY, HYBRID VOICINGS.

PRE-CHORUS

Cmaj7 B-7 Amaj7 E-7 Cmaj7 B-7 Amaj7 E-7

Cmaj7 B-7 Amaj7 E-7 Cmaj7 B-7 Amaj7 A6 A-7

CHORUS

Gmaj7 F#-7 E-11 Dmaj7 A-7 Gmaj7 F#-7 E-11 Dmaj7 A-7

Gmaj7 F#-7 E-11 Dmaj7 Cmaj7 B-7 Amaj7 E-7

1st X

Cmaj7 B-7 Amaj7 A6

TO ⊕

INTERLUDE

C#-7 B-7 Amaj7 B-7 C#-7

(GUITAR)

Amaj7 Dmaj7 C#-7 B-7 C#7b9 F#-7 1. B-7 C#-7 Cmaj9 C/F D/E 2. B7b9 E7#5 A6 D/E

Amaj7 Dmaj7 C#-7 B-7 C#7b9 F#-7 B-7 C#-7 Cmaj9 C/F D/E

CONT. SIM.

(GUITAR)

Amaj7 Dmaj7 C#-7 B-7 C#7b9 F#-7 B7b9 E7#5 1. A6 D/E 2. A6 D.S. AL ⊕

⊕ OUTRO/GUITAR SOLO

REPEAT AND FADE

Cmaj7 B-7 Amaj7 E-7 Cmaj7 B-7 Amaj7 A6

GOOD FOR IMPROVISING ON II V I PROGRESSIONS IN THREE KEY CENTERS.

TURNAROUND

(MED. BLUES)

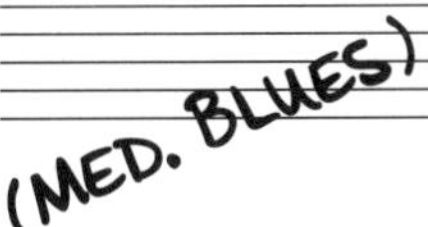

- ORNETTE COLEMAN

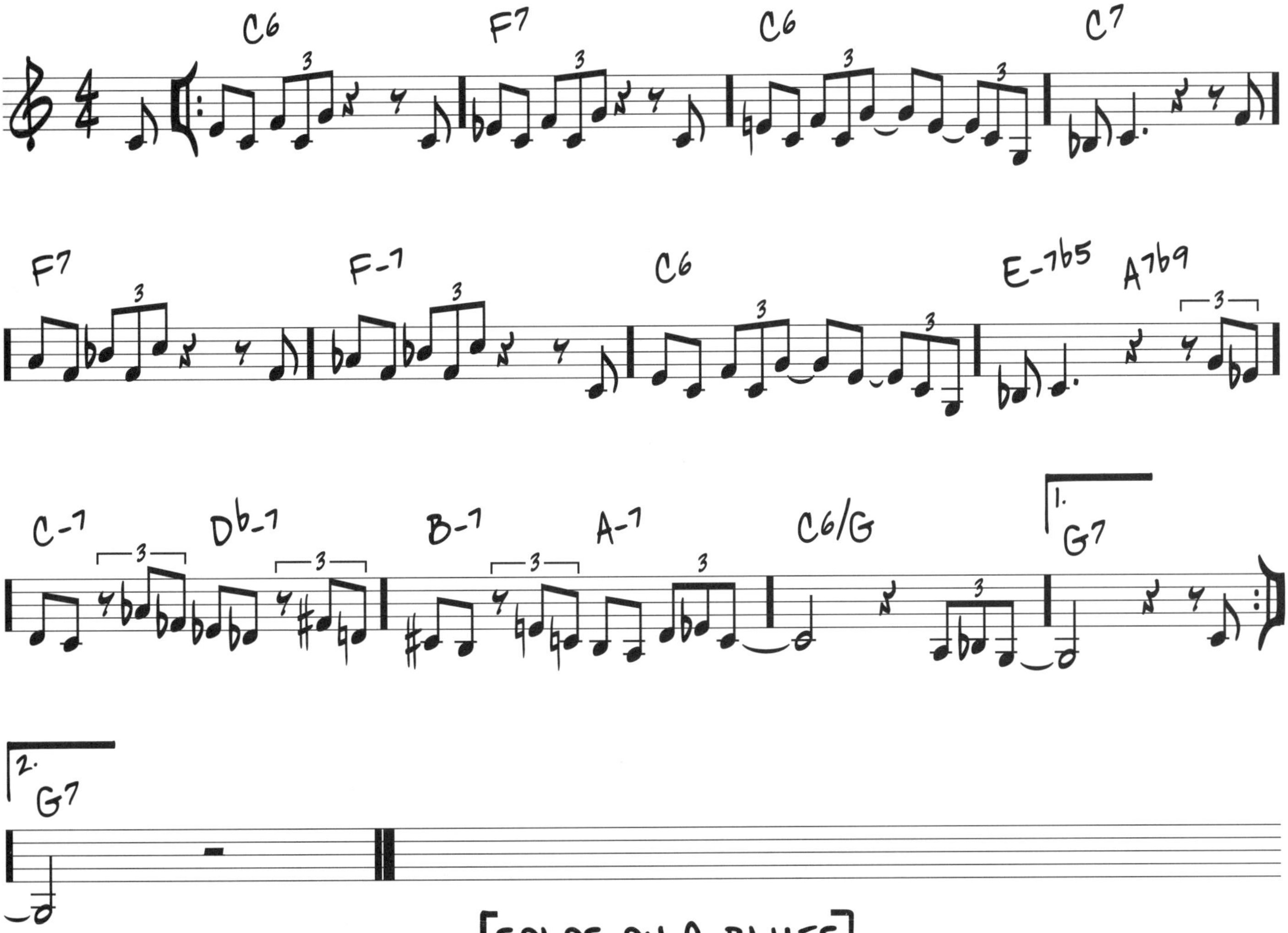
C6
F7
C6
C7
F7
F-7
C6
E-7b5
A7b9
C-7
Db-7
B-7
A-7
C6/G
1.
G7
2.
G7

[SOLOS ON C BLUES]

UP-TEMPO TUNE.

UGETSU

(UP SWING)

ART BLAKELY & THE JAZZ MESSENGERS, UGETSU, FANTASY INC., 1963.

- CEDAR WALTON

SOLO FORM A A B B
NO KICKS ON SOLOS
AFTER SOLOS, D.S. (PLAY PICKUP)
VAMP B FOR ENDING

GOOD EXAMPLE OF A JAZZ WALTZ.
UP JUMPED SPRING
(MED. JAZZ WALTZ)
FREDDIE HUBBARD, BACKLASH, ATLANTIC RECORDING CORP., 1966.
- FREDDIE HUBBARD
Bbmaj7 G7#5 C-7 F7 F#o7
G-7 F-7 E-7 A7
D-7 Eb-7 D-7 Eb-7
1. B7#11 E7 C-7b5 F7
2. C-7 F7 Bb6 A-7b5 D7
G-7 C7 Fmaj7 D-7
Ab-7 Db7 C-7 F7
Bbmaj7 G7#5 C-7 F7 F#o7
G-7 F-7 E-7 A7
D-7 Eb-7 D-7 Eb-7
C-7 F7 Bmaj7 Bbmaj7
(LAST X)

FAIRLY DIFFICULT, AABA FORM WITH TAG.

UPPER MANHATTAN MEDICAL GROUP

GOOD FOR PRACTICING IMPROVISATION IN 3/4, AND ALSO FOR USING V7/II.

SLOW-MOVING HARMONY, BEAUTIFUL CLASSIC BALLAD.

UP-TEMPO MINOR TUNE WITH ASCENDING CHROMATIC KEY SHIFTS IN BRIDGE.

VOYAGE

LISTEN TO MESSAGE OF THE SONG,
AND MAKE SURE THE BEAT SUPPORTS THAT.

VIDEO

ACOUSTIC SOUL, UNIVERSAL MOTOWN RECORDS, 2001.

- REGINALD HARGIS/CARLOS BROADY/INDIA.ARIE/SHANNON SANDERS

B-7 A-7 B-7 E-7

B-7 A-7 B-7 E-7

B-7 A-7 B-7 TO ⊕ 1., 3. E-7 2nd X, D.S. AL ⊕

2. E-7 **BRIDGE** Cmaj7 B-7 A-7

Cmaj7 B-7 A-7

Cmaj7 B-7 A-7

Cmaj7 B-7 A-7 Gmaj7 Fmaj7

⊕ ENDING: REPEAT CHORUS AS DESIRED

GOOD EXAMPLE OF LINE CLICHÉ, SECONDARY DOMINANTS, CONSTANT STRUCTURE RELATED TO DORIAN HARMONY.
VISIONS
(MED. SLOW)
INNERVISIONS, UMG RECORDINGS, INC., 1973.
- STEVIE WONDER
INTRO
B-(add9)
C#-(add9)
(GUITAR)
VERSE
A7
G13
E7#9
D7#9
F#7#5
BRIDGE
A13
G#-7b5
C#7
F#-
F#-/F
D#-7b5
G#sus4
G#

C#-(add9)
C#-/B
A#-7b5
VERSE
D#-7b5
G#
C#-
F#+
B-(add9)
C#-(add9)
B-(add9)
A13
G13
E7#9
D7#9
F#7#5
B-(add9)
C#-(add9)
B-(add9)
C#-(add9)
B-(add9)
C#-(add9)
B-(add9)
1.
C#-(add9)
D.S. AL
2.
A13
G13
E7#9
D7#9
F#7#5
B-(add9)
C#-(add9)
OUTRO-GUITAR SOLO
REPEAT AND FADE
B-(add9)
C#-(add9)
B-(add9)
C#-(add9)

SOLID, HARD-SWINGING BEBOP TUNE WITH A SUBTLE MELODY.

WABASH

(MED. SWING)

JOHN COLTRANE AND CANNONBALL ADDERLEY, CANNONBALL AND COLTRANE, POLYGRAM RECORDS, 1991 (1959).

- JULIAN ADDERLY

C6 F7 Bb7

C6 E-7 A7

D-7 G7 C6 G7b9 C6

A-7 D7 Eb-7 Ab7 D-7 G7

C6 F7 Bb7

C6 E-7 A7

D-7 G7 F-7 Bb7 E-7 A7b9

Eb-7 Ab7 D-7 G7 C6 (D-7 G7)

THE WATERGATE BLUES

(MED. SWING)

- PERCY HEATH

SINGABLE YET QUIRKY PHRASING; EXEMPLIFIES SCOFIELD'S ECLECTIC STYLE.

WABASH III

TIME ON MY HANDS, BLUE NOTE RECORDS, 1990.

- JOHN SCOFIELD

(FAST SWING)

A

F7 Bb7

(TENOR)

(GUITAR)

C7 F7

B

F7 Bb7

3 3

C7 F7

C
Bb7
C7sus4
C7
D-7
C7/E
D
F7
Bb7
C7
F7
FINE
3
3

GREAT HORN LINES.
WATERMELON MAN
HERBIE HANCOCK, CANTALOUPE ISLAND, BLUE NOTE RECORDS, 1994.
(MED. ROCK)
- HERBIE HANCOCK
INTRO
F7
HEAD
F7
RHYTHM CONT. SIM.
Bb7
F7
C7
Bb7
C7
Bb7
C7
Bb7
F7

STANDARD AABA FORM, BRIDGE MODULES TO ANOTHER KEY, ACCESSIBLE HARMONY.

THE WAY YOU LOOK TONIGHT

R & B
WE GOT IT
IMMATURE, MCA RECORDS, 1995
(MED. FUNK)
- ALLEN TOUSSAINT/CHRIS STOKES/SEAN MATHER/JUANITA CARTER
INTRO
C#-9
F#13
C#-9
F#13
(HORNS)
CHORUS
C#-9
F#13
C#-9
F#13
C#-9
F#13
C#-9
F#13
VERSE
C#-9
F#13
C#-9
F#13
C#-9
F#13
C#-9
F#13

CHORUS
C#-9
F#13
C#-9
F#13
C#-9
F#13
C#-9
1.
F#13
2.
F#13
INTERLUDE
N.C.
(BASS)
C#-9
F#13
C#-9
F#13
OUTRO-CHORUS
C#-9
F#13
C#-9
F#13
C#-9
F#13
C#-9
F#13
REPEAT AND FADE

EXCELLENT FOR WORKING ON ♭II7 CHORD, AND THE BRIDGE IS A CHALLENGE.

WELL YOU NEEDN'T
(IT'S OVER NOW)

THELONIOUS MONK, LIVE AT THE JAZZ WORKSHOP-COMPLETE, SONY, 2001 (1964).

WHAT'D I SAY
(MED. BOUNCE)
- RAY CHARLES
F
Bb9
Bb7
F7
C7
Bb7
F7
1., 2.
3.
F
Bb7
F
C7
Bb7
F
1.
2.

ONE OF THE BEST R&B STANDARDS, WITH SOPHISTICATED CHANGES.

CHORUS
F♯-7
A/B
F♯-7
A/B
F♯-7
A/B
E maj7
C♯-7
E maj7
C♯-7
TO ⊕
INTERLUDE W/AD LIB. SCAT VOCALS
A-9
(INSTRUMENTAL BACKGROUND)
D.S. AL ⊕
(TAKE 2nd ENDING)
A/B
⊕ OUTRO
A-9
(AS BEFORE)
A/B
REPEAT AND FADE

NICE BALLAD, WITH II V MOTION AND SEQUENTIAL KEY CHANGE AT THE BRIDGE.

CHARACTERIZED BY THE DESCENDING HARMONIC LINE-CLICHÉ IN THE A SECTION.

WHISPER NOT

ART BLAKEY, JAZZ IN PARIS, 1958 OLYMPIA, SSC, 2001 (1958).

(MED.)

- BENNY GOLSON

A SIMPLE MOTIVIC MELODY THAT DEVELOPS THROUGH HARMONIC MOTION.

WHO CAN I TURN TO
(WHEN NOBODY NEEDS ME)

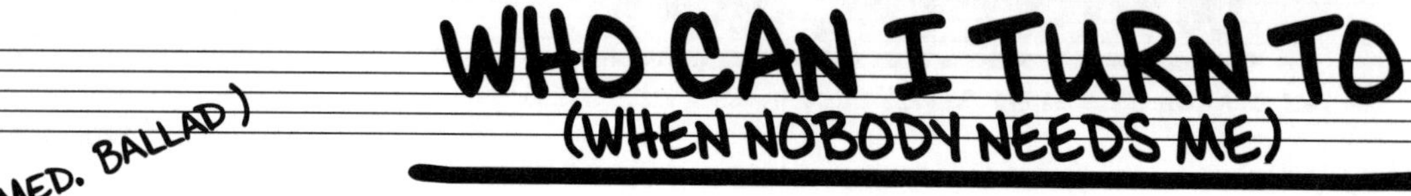

(MED. BALLAD)

BILL EVANS, BILL EVANS AT TOWN HALL, VERVE MUSIC GROUP, 1966.

- LESLIE BRICUSSE/ANTHONY NEWLEY

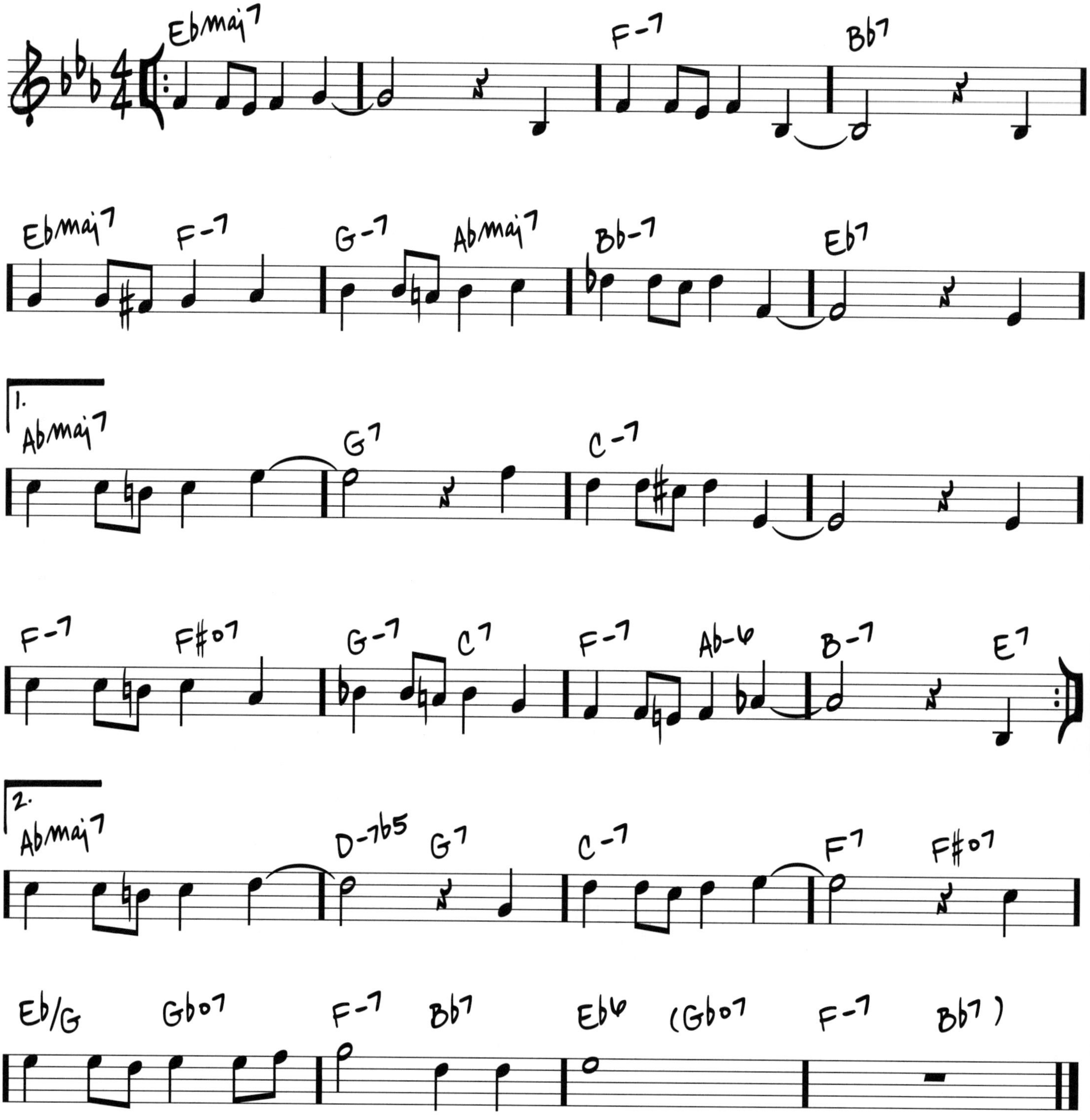
Ebmaj7 F-7 Bb7
Ebmaj7 F-7 G-7 Abmaj7 Bb-7 Eb7
1. Abmaj7 G7 C-7
F-7 F#o7 G-7 C7 F-7 Ab-6 B-7 E7
2. Abmaj7 D-7b5 G7 C-7 F7 F#o7
Eb/G Gbo7 F-7 Bb7 Eb6 (Gbo7 F-7 Bb7)

CLASSIC BLUESY BALLAD.

WITCH HUNT

(MED. JAZZ)

WAYNE SHORTER, SPEAK NO EVIL, BLUE NOTE RECORDS, 1999 (1964).

- WAYNE SHORTER

INTRO

N.C. Ebmaj7 Fmaj7 N.C. Gmaj7 Dmaj7 N.C.

Amaj7 Bmaj7 Gbmaj7 Abmaj7 Dbmaj7 (IN TIME)

C-7

HEAD

C-7 G7#9 C-7 G7#9

C-7 G7#9 C-7

Eb7 G7#9

GOOD EXAMPLE OF SEQUENTIAL MINOR II V'S, BEBOP CLASSIC.

EXTREMELY SIMPLE, YET EFFECTIVE, RHYTHM SECTION ARRANGING.

D/F# C D (E- D7/F# /A) 2. G
BRIDGE
C D G D/F# E-
C D C D
INTERLUDE
G D/F# C D (E- D7/F# /A)
D.S. AL
G D/F# C D (E- D7/F# /A)
G D/F# E- D C D
OUTRO
G D/F# C D (E- D7/F# /A)
G D/F# C D (E- D7/F# /A)
RIT.

(MED.)

WORK SONG

- NAT ADDERLY

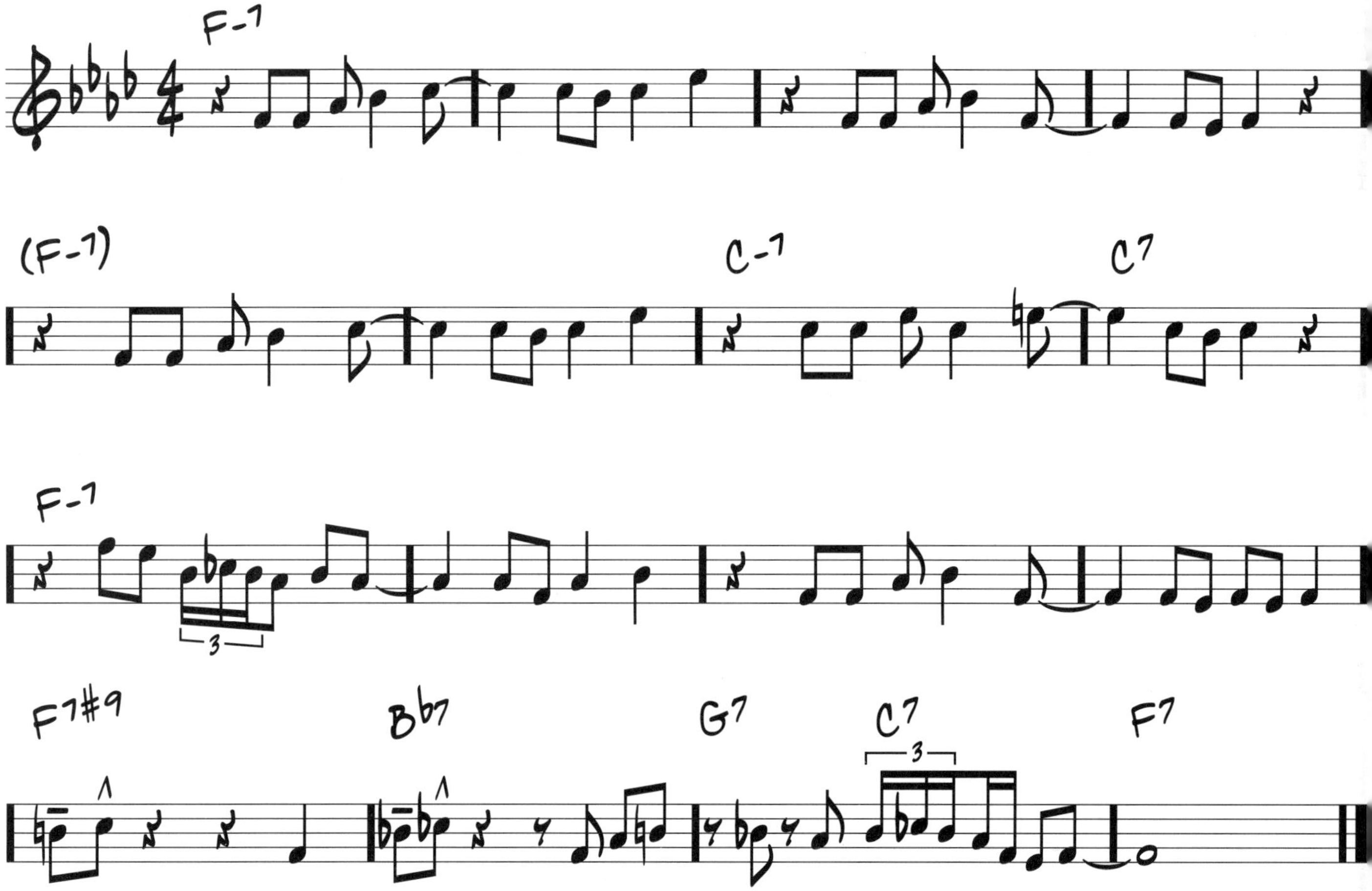

F-7

(F-7) C-7 C7

F-7

F7#9 Bb7 G7 C7 F7

EXAMPLES OF DIRECT MODULATION, DORIAN MODE, AEOLIAN INTERCHANGE, HYBRID CHORDS, BASS OSTINATO.

X MARKS THE SPOT
(MARIE LAVEAU)

THE PECAN TREE, PRA RECORDS, 2002.

- JOE SAMPLE

BEBOP, AABA FORM, HARMONICALLY INTERESTING.
YARDBIRD SUITE
(MED. UP)
CHARLIE PARKER, THE GENIUS OF CHARLIE PARKER, SAVOY JAZZ, 1945.
- CHARLIE PARKER
C6 F-7 Bb7 Cmaj7 Bb7 A7
D7 G7 E-7 A7 D-7 G7
G7 C6 F#-7b5 B7b9
E-7 F#-7b5 B7b9 E-7 A7
D-7 E-7 A7 D7 D-7 G7
C6 F-7 Bb7 Cmaj7 Bb7 A7
TO
D7 D-7 G7 C6 D-7 G7
AFTER SOLOS, D.C. AL
(TAKE REPEAT)
D-7 G7 Cmaj7

CHROMATIC MELODY LEADS INTO VI CHORD.

SECONDARY DOMINANTS, TONIC MINOR MODAL INTERCHANGE, WHOLE TONE CHORD SCALE, MODULATIONS, HYBRID VOICING, POLYCHORD VOICING.

YOU ARE THE SUNSHINE OF MY LIFE

STEVIE WONDER, TALKING BOOK, MOTOWN RECORDS, 1972.

(ROCK) - STEVIE WONDER

CHORUS
C
G/F
E-7
A7b9
D-7
G7sus4
C
D-7
G7
C
G/F
E-7
A7b9
D-7
G7sus4
C
D-7
G7
D.S. FOR SOLOS
Cmaj7
(ENDING)

A TRADITIONAL JAZZ STANDARD CENTERED IN MINOR KEY THAT WORKS WELL IN 7/4 TOO.

YOU DON'T KNOW WHAT LOVE IS

WYNTON MARSALIS, LIVE AT THE HOUSE OF TRIBES, BLUE NOTE RECORDS, 2005.

- DON RAYE/GENE DEPAUL

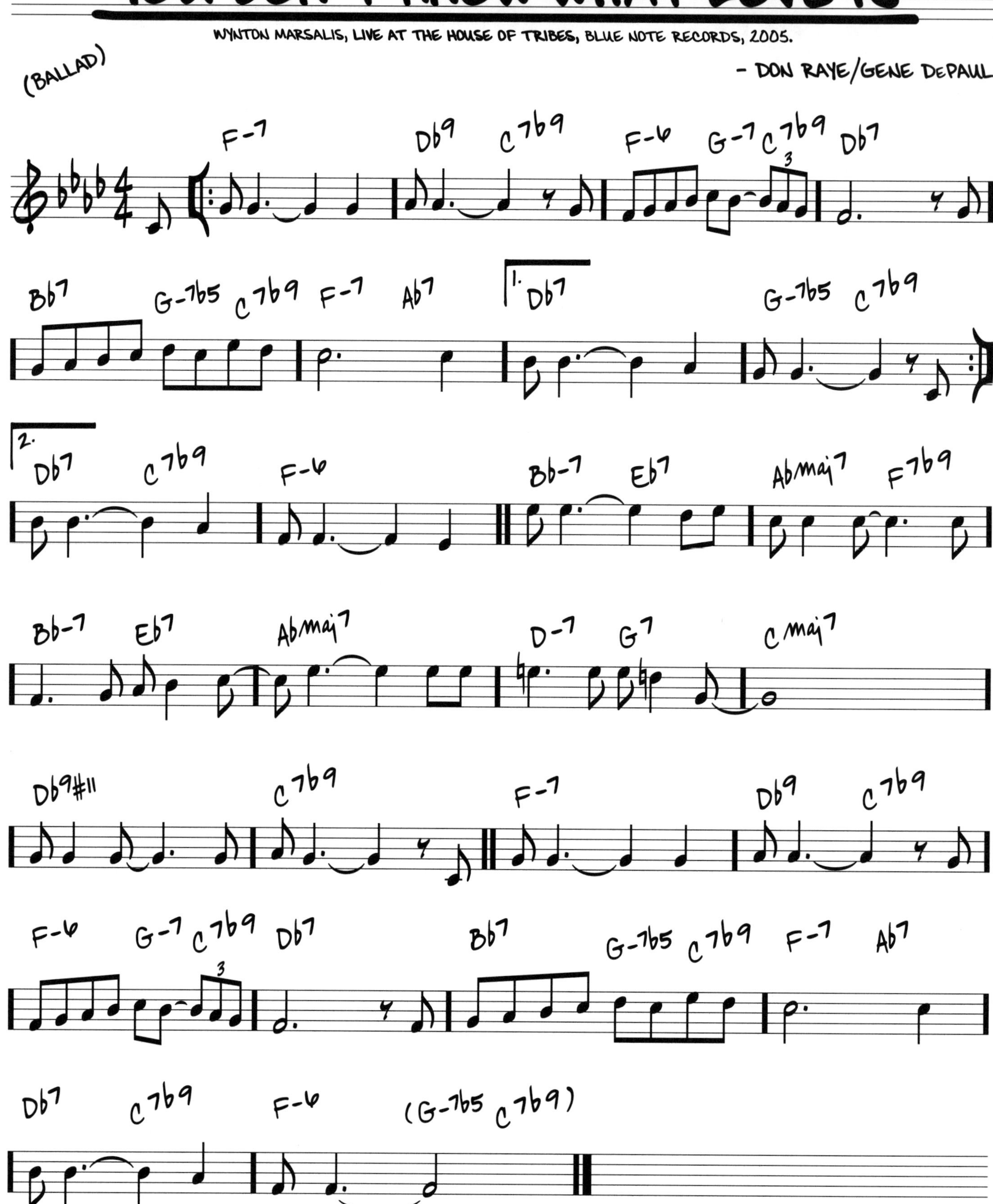

USED TO PRACTICE REHARMONIZATION. BASIC CHORDS PROVIDED.

YOU'RE MY EVERYTHING

(MED.)

MILES DAVIS QUINTET, RELAXIN' WITH THE MILES DAVIS QUINTET, PRESTIGE, 2006.

- MORT DIXON/JOE YOUNG/HARRY WARREN

EXAMPLE OF '90S POP CONSTRUCTION.

YOU MEAN THE WORLD TO ME

D#- | Dmaj7 D6 | F#

C-7b5 | G#-7 | 1. Dmaj7 B/C# N.C.

2. Dmaj7 B/C#

BRIDGE

A#7 | D#-7

G#-7 | B/C# C#/B | A#7

D#-7 | G#-7

OUTRO-CHORUS

Dmaj7 B/C# | F#

F#/E | D#- | Dmaj7 D6

REPEAT AND FADE

F# | C-7b5 | G#-7 | B/C#

More Fine Publications

GUITAR

BERKLEE ESSENTIAL GUITAR SONGBOOK
Kim Perlak, Sheryl Bailey, and Members of the Berklee Guitar Department Faculty
00350814 Book $22.99

BERKLEE GUITAR CHORD DICTIONARY
Rick Peckham
50449546 Jazz – Book $16.99
50449596 Rock – Book $12.99

BERKLEE GUITAR STYLE STUDIES
Jim Kelly
00200377 Book/Online Media $24.99

BERKLEE GUITAR THEORY
Kim Perlak and Members of the Berklee Guitar Department Faculty
00276326 Book $26.99

BLUES GUITAR TECHNIQUE
Michael Williams
50449623 Book/Online Audio $29.99

CLASSICAL TECHNIQUE FOR THE MODERN GUITARIST
Kim Perlak
00148781 Book/Online Audio $19.99

COUNTRY GUITAR STYLES
Mike Ihde
00254157 Book/Online Audio $24.99

CREATIVE CHORDAL HARMONY FOR GUITAR
Mick Goodrick & Tim Miller
50449613 Book/Online Audio $24.99

FUNK/R&B GUITAR
Thaddeus Hogarth
50449569 Book/Online Audio $25.99

GUITAR SWEEP PICKING
Joe Stump
00151223 Book/Online Audio $24.99

JAZZ GUITAR FRETBOARD NAVIGATION
Mark White
00154107 Book/Online Audio $24.99

MODAL VOICINGS FOR GUITAR
Rick Peckham
00151227 Book/Online Media $24.99

A MODERN METHOD FOR GUITAR – VOLUMES 1-3 COMPLETE*
William Leavitt
00292990 Book/Online Media $54.99
**Individual volumes, media options, and supporting songbooks available.*

A MODERN METHOD FOR GUITAR SCALES
Larry Baione
00199318 Book $15.99

TRIADS FOR THE IMPROVISING GUITARIST
Jane Miller
00284857 Book/Online Audio $22.99

BASS

BERKLEE JAZZ BASS
Rich Appleman, Whit Browne & Bruce Gertz
50449636 Book/Online Audio $25.99

CHORD STUDIES FOR ELECTRIC BASS
Rich Appleman & Joseph Viola
50449750 Book $24.99

FUNK BASS FILLS
Anthony Vitti
50449608 Book/Online Audio $24.99

INSTANT BASS
Danny Morris
50449502 Book/CD $9.99

METAL BASS LINES
David Marvuglio
00122465 Book/Online Audio $19.99

READING CONTEMPORARY ELECTRIC BASS
Rich Appleman
50449770 Book $24.99

PIANO/KEYBOARD

BERKLEE JAZZ KEYBOARD HARMONY
Suzanna Sifter
00138874 Book/Online Audio $29.99

BERKLEE JAZZ PIANO
Ray Santisi
50448047 Book/Online Audio $24.99

BERKLEE JAZZ STANDARDS FOR SOLO PIANO
Robert Christopherson, Hey Rim Jeon, Ross Ramsay, Tim Ray
00160482 Book/Online Audio $24.99

CHORD-SCALE IMPROVISATION FOR KEYBOARD
Ross Ramsay
50449597 Book/CD $19.99

CONTEMPORARY PIANO TECHNIQUE
Stephany Tiernan
50449545 Book/DVD $39.99

HAMMOND ORGAN COMPLETE
Dave Limina
00237801 Book/Online Audio $27.99

JAZZ PIANO COMPING
Suzanne Davis
50449614 Book/Online Audio $26.99

LATIN JAZZ PIANO IMPROVISATION
Rebecca Cline
50449649 Book/Online Audio $29.99

PIANO ESSENTIALS
Ross Ramsay
50448046 Book/Online Audio $26.99

SOLO JAZZ PIANO
Neil Olmstead
50449641 Book/Online Audio $42.99

Berklee Press publications feature material developed at Berklee College of Music.
To browse the complete Berklee Press Catalog, go to **www.berkleepress.com**

DRUMS

BEGINNING DJEMBE
Michael Markus & Joe Galeota
00148210 Book/Online Video $16.99

BERKLEE JAZZ DRUMS
Casey Scheuerell
50449612 Book/Online Audio $27.99

DRUM SET WARM-UPS
Rod Morgenstein
50449465 Book $16.99

A MANUAL FOR THE MODERN DRUMMER
Alan Dawson & Don DeMichael
50449560 Book $14.99

MASTERING THE ART OF BRUSHES
Jon Hazilla
50449459 Book/Online Audio $19.99

PHRASING
Russ Gold
00120209 Book/Online Media $19.99

WORLD JAZZ DRUMMING
Mark Walker
50449568 Book/CD $27.99

BERKLEE PRACTICE METHOD

GET YOUR BAND TOGETHER
With additional volumes for other instruments, plus a teacher's guide.

Drum Set
Ron Savage, Casey Scheuerell and the Berklee Faculty
50449429 Book/CD $19.99

Guitar
Larry Baione and the Berklee Faculty
50449426 Book/CD $29.99

Keyboard
Russell Hoffmann, Paul Schmeling and the Berklee Faculty
50449428 Book/Online Audio $22.99

VOICE

BELTING
Jeannie Gagné
00124984 Book/Online Media $24.99

THE CONTEMPORARY SINGER
Anne Peckham
50449595 Book/Online Audio $29.99

JAZZ VOCAL IMPROVISATION
Mili Bermejo
00159290 Book/Online Audio $19.99

TIPS FOR SINGERS
Carolyn Wilkins
50449557 Book/CD $19.95

VOCAL WORKOUTS FOR THE CONTEMPORARY SINGER
Anne Peckham
50448044 Book/Online Audio $27.99

YOUR SINGING VOICE
Jeannie Gagné
50449619 Book/Online Audio $34.99

WOODWINDS & BRASS

TRUMPET SOUND EFFECTS
Craig Pederson & Ueli Dörig
00121626 Book/Online Audio $14.99

SAXOPHONE SOUND EFFECTS
Ueli Dörig
50449628 Book/Online Audio.................$22.99

THE TECHNIQUE OF THE FLUTE
Joseph Viola
00214012 Book..$19.99

STRINGS/ROOTS MUSIC

BERKLEE HARP
Felice Pomeranz
00144263 Book/Online Audio..................$26.99

BEYOND BLUEGRASS BANJO
Dave Hollander & Matt Glaser
50449610 Book/CD $19.99

BEYOND BLUEGRASS MANDOLIN
John McGann & Matt Glaser
50449609 Book/CD $19.99

BLUEGRASS FIDDLE & BEYOND
Matt Glaser
50449602 Book/CD $19.99

CONTEMPORARY CELLO ETUDES
Mike Block
00159292 Book/Online Audio $24.99

EXPLORING CLASSICAL MANDOLIN
August Watters
00125040 Book/Online Media.................$24.99

THE IRISH CELLO BOOK
Liz Davis Maxfield
50449652 Book/Online Audio.................$29.99

JAZZ UKULELE
Abe Lagrimas, Jr.
00121624 Book/Online Audio..................$26.99

MUSIC THEORY & EAR TRAINING

BEGINNING EAR TRAINING
Gilson Schachnik
50449548 Book/Online Audio.................$22.99

BERKLEE CONTEMPORARY MUSIC NOTATION
Jonathan Feist
00202547 Book $27.99

BERKLEE MUSIC THEORY
Paul Schmeling
50449615 Book 1/Online Audio...............$29.99
50449616 Book 2/Online Audio...............$26.99

CONTEMPORARY COUNTERPOINT
Beth Denisch
00147050 Book/Online Audio..................$24.99

MUSIC NOTATION
Mark McGrain
50449399 Book..$29.99
Matthew Nicholl & Richard Grudzinski
50449540 Book $25.99

REHARMONIZATION TECHNIQUES
Randy Felts
50449496 Book $29.99

CONDUCTING

CONDUCTING MUSIC TODAY
Bruce Hangen
00237719 Book/Online Media..................$24.99

MUSIC PRODUCTION & ENGINEERING

AUDIO MASTERING
Jonathan Wyner
50449581 Book/CD $34.99

AUDIO POST PRODUCTION
Mark Cross
50449627 Book...$32.99

CREATING COMMERCIAL MUSIC
Peter Bell
00278535 Book/Online Media $19.99

HIP-HOP PRODUCTION
Prince Charles Alexander
50449582 Book/Online Audio.................$24.99

THE SINGER-SONGWRITER'S GUIDE TO RECORDING IN THE HOME STUDIO
Shane Adams
00148211 Book...$24.99

UNDERSTANDING AUDIO
Daniel M. Thompson
00148197 Book...$49.99

MUSIC BUSINESS

CROWDFUNDING FOR MUSICIANS
Laser Malena-Webber
00285092 Book...$17.99

ENGAGING THE CONCERT AUDIENCE
David Wallace
00244532 Book/Online Media.................$24.99

HOW TO GET A JOB IN THE MUSIC INDUSTRY
Keith Hatschek with Breanne Beseda
00130699 Book...$39.99

MAKING MUSIC MAKE MONEY
Eric Beall
00355740 Book $29.99

MUSIC INDUSTRY FORMS
Jonathan Feist
00121814 Book...$17.99

MUSIC LAW IN THE DIGITAL AGE
Allen Bargfrede
00366048 Book $29.99

MUSIC MARKETING
Mike King
50449588 Book...$24.99

PROJECT MANAGEMENT FOR MUSICIANS
Jonathan Feist
50449659 Book...$39.99

ARRANGING & IMPROVISATION

ARRANGING FOR HORNS
Jerry Gates
00121625 Book/Online Audio....................$24.99

BERKLEE BOOK OF JAZZ HARMONY
Joe Mulholland & Tom Hojnacki
00113755 Book/Online Audio....................$34.99

MODERN JAZZ VOICINGS
Ted Pease & Ken Pullig
50449485 Book/Online Audio.................$29.99

Prices subject to change without notice. Visit your local music dealer or bookstore, or go to **www.berkleepress.com**

SONGWRITING/COMPOSING

BEGINNING SONGWRITING
Andrea Stolpe with Jan Stolpe
00138503 Book/Online Audio..................$22.99

COMPLETE GUIDE TO FILM SCORING
Richard Davis
50449607 Book $39.99

THE CRAFT OF SONGWRITING
Scarlet Keys
00159283 Book/Online Audio $24.99

CREATIVE STRATEGIES IN FILM SCORING
Ben Newhouse
00242911 Book/Online Media...................$27.99

JAZZ COMPOSITION
Ted Pease
50448000 Book/Online Audio $49.99

MELODY IN SONGWRITING
Jack Perricone
50449419 Book...$26.99

MUSIC COMPOSITION FOR FILM AND TELEVISION
Lalo Schifrin
50449604 Book...$39.99

POPULAR LYRIC WRITING
Andrea Stolpe
50449553 Book $17.99

THE SONGWRITER'S WORKSHOP
Jimmy Kachulis
Harmony
50449519 Book/Online Audio $34.99
Melody
50449518 Book/Online Audio $27.99

SONGWRITING: ESSENTIAL GUIDE
Pat Pattison
Lyric Form and Structure
50481582 Book...$22.99
Rhyming
00124366 Book...$24.99

SONGWRITING IN PRACTICE
Mark Simos
00244545 Book...$16.99

SONGWRITING STRATEGIES
Mark Simos
50449621 Book...$27.99

SONGBOOKS

NEW STANDARDS
Terri Lyne Carrington
00369515 Book $29.99

WELLNESS/AUTOBIOGRAPHY

LEARNING TO LISTEN: THE JAZZ JOURNEY OF GARY BURTON
Gary Burton
00117798 Book...$34.99

MANAGE YOUR STRESS AND PAIN THROUGH MUSIC
Dr. Suzanne B. Hanser & Dr. Susan E. Mandel
50449592 Book/Online Audio $34.99

MUSICIAN'S YOGA
Mia Olson
50449587 Book...$26.99

NEW MUSIC THERAPIST'S HANDBOOK
Dr. Suzanne B. Hanser
00279325 Book...$34.99

0820
179